Out of Your Mind... and Into the Marketplace™

by

LINDA PINSON
&
JERRY JINNETT

Published by

OUT OF YOUR MIND . . .
AND INTO THE MARKETPLACE™
Fullerton, CA 92633

OUT OF YOUR MIND...
   AND INTO THE MARKETPLACE™ by Linda Pinson and Jerry Jinnett

First Printing, 1987
Second printing, revised, 1988

Published by: Out of Your Mind...
                        and into the Marketplace™
               3031 Colt Way #223
               Fullerton, CA 92633

©1987 and 1988 Linda Pinson and Jerry Jinnett

All rights reserved. No part of this book may be reproduced or transmitted in any form with the intention of reselling such copies without written permission from the publisher, except for brief quotations included in a review.

Buyers of this book are licensed to use the forms included in this book in the course of conducting their own businesses. The contents of this book, however, may not be reproduced for sale.

This book was written with the understanding that the authors are not engaged in rendering legal or accounting service. The information included in this book has been carefully prepared and is correct to the best of our knowledge as of publication date. If you require legal or expert advice, the services of professionals should be used. The authors disclaim any personal liability, either directly or indirectly, for advice or information presented in this book.

Library of Congress Catalog Card No: 87-91959

ISBN 0-944205-08-9

Printed in the United States of America

INTRODUCTION

This book has been written in the hopes that it will provide the small and home-based business entrepreneur with all the information, forms and worksheets needed for business start-up and development into a successful operation.

We have tried to present the information in a logical sequence. You will find, however, that many segments of business overlap. We would suggest that you read the whole book through one time and then go back and begin with the process of forming your business. At the end of the text in each chapter, we have included various forms, samples, and worksheets which you should find to be helpful. We hope this book will be useful as you progress through various stages of your business. Feel free to duplicate any of the pages for your own use, but not for commercial use.

We have written this book out of our own experiences. Having been friends for many years, we have encouraged each other through many business and non-business ventures. Sometimes, only a sense of humor has kept us going, but all of our experiences were beneficial and sources of knowledge. We hope that you enjoy the book and that it provides you with the motivation and knowledge to take your idea **OUT OF YOUR MIND...AND INTO THE MARKETPLACE**™!!!

TABLE OF CONTENTS

1. **FINDING A BUSINESS** .... page 1

2. **CHOOSING A BUSINESS NAME** .... page 7

3. **PRESENTING YOUR BUSINESS** .... page 11
   Business Cards, Stationery, Brochures .... page 17-23

4. **PROTECTING YOUR BUSINESS** .... page 25
   Copyright… .... page 28
   Trademark… .... page 29
   Patents… .... page 30
   Addresses of Federal Agencies… .... page 33

5. **LEGAL STRUCTURES** .... page 35
   Sole Proprietorship .... page 37
   Partnership .... page 38
   Partnership Agreement .... page 39
   Corporation .... page 40
   Subchapter S .... page 41
   Certificate of Incorporation .... page 42
   Resources .... page 44

6. **SECURING A BUSINESS LICENSE** .... page 51

7. **REGISTERING A FICTITIOUS NAME (DBA)** .... page 55

8. **HOME-BASED BUSINESS** .... page 61

9. **OBTAINING A SELLER'S PERMIT** .... page 65
   Resale Certificate .... page 68
   Reporting Sales Tax Collected .... page 68
   Sample Forms and Chart .... pages 71-77

10. **SETTING UP A BANK ACCOUNT** .... page 79

11. **FINANCING YOUR BUSINESS** .... **page 85**
    Operating Expenses .... page 88
    Cost of Goods Sold .... page 90
    Hourly Rate Formula .... page 91
    Formula For Manufacturers .... page 92

12. **KEEPING RECORDS** .... **page 101**
    General Journal, Other Records .... pages 104-107
    Recordkeeping Schedule .... page 109
    Worksheets .... pages 110-133

13. **SELECTING YOUR INSURANCE** .... **page 135**

14. **MARKETING YOUR BUSINESS** .... **page 141**
    Market Research .... page 144
    Market Planning .... page 147
    Market Worksheets .... page 151-157

15. **ADVERTISING YOUR BUSINESS** .... **page 159**
    Media Publicity .... page 161
    Displays, Community, Networking .... page 162
    Trade Shows & Exhibits .... page 163
    Direct Mail .... page 163
    Yellow Pages .... page 163
    Discounts .... page 163
    Promotional Gimmicks .... page 163
    Advertising Worksheets .... pages 166-169

16. **BUSINESS PLANNING** .... **page 171**
    Purpose .... page 173
    Format .... page 174
    Revision .... page 174
    Information Resources .... page 175
    Anatomy of a Business Plan .... page 175

17. **FOR MORE INFORMATION** .... **pages 177-183**

1.

FINDING A BUSINESS

1. FINDING A BUSINESS

Everyone has dreamed of having a business of his or her own. At one time or another, we all have ideas that come into our minds but never quite make it into the marketplace. It has been said that an entrepreneur can best be defined by the following thought: All people have great ideas while in the shower. Most of us get out of the shower and forget about them. The entrepreneur is the person who gets out and acts on those ideas.

It is important to learn that you may very well have the skills and interests necessary to provide a new service or create a new product. Take a close look at your skills and your areas of interest. Skills are abilities to use one's knowledge proficiently. Your interests are those things which you enjoy doing and which bring you pleasure.

A **Skills and Interest Worksheet** has been provided to help you evaluate your potential. Keep this worksheet within easy reach and fill it out as you go along. You may have everyday skills and interests that could be enhanced and utilized for business purposes. Do you enjoy working with other people? If so, you could consider tutoring or teaching a skill. Do you have mechanical ability? You might consider a repair service. Are you interested in arts and crafts? You can turn what has been a hobby into a full-scale business. After you have filled out the Skills and Interest columns on your worksheet, you are ready to tackle the third column, Business Possibilities. This column is filled out by evaluating and combining the other two. For example, if one of your interests is dining out and you have writing skills, you can write and publish a dining guide. If you collect music boxes and have mechanical skills, you can provide a music box service combining repairs and sales. We would like to suggest that you place extra emphasis on the interest area, as you will be spending a great deal of time in your business pursuit and you might as well enjoy it. The ability to do well at your business may prove to be rewarding while the business is new, but if you do not like your work, it soon becomes a drudgery. Instead of looking forward to beginning your business day, you will be searching for a way to escape to a more interesting occupation.

Now that you have an idea for a business, take classes to learn all that you can about your chosen field. Find a job in your field of interest. If you are interested in catering or some other facet of the food industry, work at a restaurant. Learn all the aspects of the business. How are supplies ordered, how are deliveries handled, how is inventory controlled, how is food handled, and what does an invoice look like? What methods work? What would you improve? You are not going to steal their business plan. You are getting an education while earning extra money to put toward your business. You will learn to feel comfortable with the terminologies and procedures of the food industry. You will also find out if you really enjoy working with food.

An entrepreneur can do one of two things. He or she can either develop a new product or improve an existing one. Now is the time for the old adage, "Find a need and fill it". New products are usually spawned out of the imagination. If you can't think of something new, it is well to remember that many products can be improved upon. A man I know has designed an improved version of a jack for leveling mobile homes. He is a welder, and in addition to designing the jack, he is also the manufacturer. He has created a double need for his talents. His product is timely and today he is a busy, happy and PROSPEROUS man!

Your interests may be more in the area of providing a service. A perfect example of this is the X-ray technician who saw a need for mobile x-ray units. He started with one and, at the last count, had eight fully-equipped vans serving a large area.

The most important consideration in selecting your business is that of making the proper choice. At this point, that choice is not written in stone. You may think that you have found the perfect business, only to discover at some point further on, that you will have to make some changes in order to proceed with it. Don't become discouraged. Few businesses end up as they were originally conceived. After completing the work in this section, you will have refined your idea. It is **OUT OF YOUR MIND...**Now, let's proceed to get it **INTO THE MARKETPLACE!!!!**

OUT OF YOUR MIND....
AND INTO THE MARKETPLACE™
SMALL & HOME-BASED BUSINESS CONSULTING

SKILLS/INTEREST WORKSHEET

SKILLS	INTERESTS	BUSINESS POSSIBILITIES

Finding a Business

2.

CHOOSING A BUSINESS NAME

2. CHOOSING A BUSINESS NAME

Now that you have decided what your business will be, you must choose your business name. The name you chose will have a great deal of bearing on the image you project. Before deciding on that name, it would be well to consider the following points:

1. Avoid cute and clever names. They do not project a business-like image. Many wholesalers will not view your operation as a legitimate business even though you may be running a full-scale enterprise.

2. Make the name descriptive to advertise your product or service. That way the consumer who sees your name will immediately associate it with the product or service you provide. For example, the name 'Royal Office Supply' tells me that you are in the office supply business. The word 'Royal' has a ring of quality and stability.

3. Keep your business name short and pronounceable. Complicated names are harder to remember.

4. Do not make your name so specific that you cannot expand your business without that name losing its descriptive quality. If you have a repair service and plan to expand into sales, you will not want to name your business 'Bob's T.V. Repair'. This would require a name change if your customers are to know at a glance that you also sell T.V.'s.

5. Consider the alphabetical listing in advertising directories. Most consumers look at the first few listings under a heading when using a business directory. You may want to be in the A's instead of the Z's.

6. There may be some advantages to using your own name as part of your business name. If you are already well-thought-of in your community or respected in your field of interest, you may wish to include you own name. This might give you a headstart into the business world. You may also wish to use your own name if you do not want to have to file a DBA. This stands for **'Doing Business As'** and is covered in the section titled **Registering a Fictitious Name**. Check the name availability with the City or County Clerk and with the Office of Name Availability, Secretary of State as discussed in the following section of this book, entitled **Legal Structures**.

Choosing a business name is a very personal matter. Do not rush your decision. Take time to choose a name with which you will be comfortable and one which will project the desired image. From the time you advertise your business name, it will be in the public eye. Select it with care and it will serve you well.

3.
PRESENTING YOUR BUSINESS

3. PRESENTING YOUR BUSINESS

From the very first day that you begin business, it will be necessary for you to have certain items to present that business—not only to your clients, but to other people in the trade. When you are trying to organize, you will be approaching suppliers, dealers and other people in related businesses. It is important that they perceive your business as having a base of stability. Otherwise, they may choose to ignore your business requests. It is almost impossible to do the groundwork that needs to be done without having business cards and letterheads. Sometimes you will also need a flyer of some type to begin advertising your business.

BUSINESS CARDS

Be sure to have business cards printed as soon as possible. Whenever you attempt to deal with another business or individual, you should give him your business card. This not only gives your business credibility, but the recipient now has a visual reminder of you and your business. It can be very difficult to design a card on demand. In a very short time, you may want to change it for any number of reasons (change of address, addition of logo, change of business name, etc.). Do not buy your first cards in great quantities. One thousand cards will do you no good if the information is no longer valid—even if you did get them at a quantity price.

Examine the business card samples at the end of this text and evaluate them in terms of the following questions:

1. What is it about this card that first draws your attention?
2. Is the logo appropriate and descriptive?
3. Is the company name legible?
4. Does the card tell you the contact person's name and phone number?
5. Does the card tell what product is offered?

6. Does it tell the service provided?
7. Does the card tell the location of the business?
8. Is the overall appearance pleasing?
9. Is the card one you will remember?

Ask these same questions of your own card as you design it.

LOGOS

A logo is a surefire way to get people to notice and remember your business. When designing your logo, you will do well to be sure that it is appropriate and that the art work is timely. Your logo can and probably will be used extensively. You can design your own, select from standard ones available at the printer's, or hire a professional artist to design one. Be sure to consider the registering of your logo either with the Copyright Office or the Patent and Trademark Office in Washington D.C. You can write directly to them for their guidelines and application forms. The address of these offices can be found at the end of the chapter titled **Protecting Your Business.**

LETTERHEADS AND ENVELOPES

Your letterhead is your business stationery. It should be used for all business correspondence and, as with your cards, lends credibility to your business. It may also contain your logo and must contain your business address and phone number. When you have your letterheads printed, purchase a smaller quantity of second sheets. When writing a business letter, the letterhead is used only for the first page.

BROCHURES

Brochure is a general term for promotional material which tells the following about your business:

1. The business name
2. The business address
3. Telephone number (include the area code)
4. Name of the contact person
5. Photos or drawings of your product
6. Description of your product or service
7. Price list
8. Terms of payment

    a. Net 30 - Invoice must be paid in full within 30 days

    b. C.O.D. - Invoice is paid to the delivery agent on receipt of goods

    c. ProForma - Goods will be shipped after receipt of full payment

9. Return policy
10. Shipping terms (F.O.B. origin would mean that the customer pays shipping charges and assumes the responsibility for the goods from the time they leave your business.)
11. Minimum order policy
12. Any warranties and guarantees offered by you

Note: Please see the sample **Business Brochure** after the text.

CHOOSING A PRINTER

Obviously, all the previously-mentioned presentation materials will have to be done at a print shop. Selecting a printer should be undertaken with a few things in mind. The two major considerations are quality and price. Some printers specialize in instant service. They are not always the most reasonable. You may be paying a premium for fast service. Quality varies greatly from one shop to another. You will want to visit two or three printers in your area. Get a price list and some samples of their work. You may have some items done at one place and some done at another that specializes in certain kinds of printed matter. For instance, the shop that does your business cards may not do layouts for more complicated presentation materials.

In order to save money, much of your printing can be done from camera-ready copy. This means that you take the printer a finished product ready to be reproduced by him. It should be noted here that camera-ready copy should only be used if you can make your layout look professional and businesslike. A poorly done piece of printed matter can be more harmful than helpful to your business.

Before having your printing done, be sure to get a written quotation. A friend of mine was given a verbal quote for printing booklets and boxes. Upon delivery, she paid the bill in full. A month later, she was surprised to receive another bill for setup charges. The printer's claim was that the setup charges were separate and that she had agreed to pay them as such. She consulted an attorney and the outcome was that she was legally responsible for the additional charges. Since there was no written agreement, she was unable to prove her claim.

IN SUMMARY

The above-mentioned are the main presentation materials used for a small business. As your business grows, you may want to develop other materials. If you are a retailer, you may decide to have a catalogue printed and mailed to your customers. You may even want to go into color processing or more elaborate methods of duplication. For the small business just starting up, business cards, letterheads, and a basic flyer or brochure are enough to get the business off to a good start.

BROCHURE SAMPLE (REVERSE SIDE)

reply card

PLEASE SEND MORE INFORMATION ON:

☐ Workshops & Seminars

☐ Textbooks

☐ Cassettes

☐ I would like to be on your mailing list.

Name _____

Address _____

City _____

State _____ Zip ___

TURN YOUR IDEA INTO A PROFITABLE BUSINESS!

OUT OF YOUR MIND...AND INTO THE MARKETPLACE™ is a small-business consulting firm whose purpose is to provide the aspiring entrepreneur with the information necessary to turn an idea into a successful and marketable business.

Let us share our Knowledge and Experience with You!

WE OFFER —

SEMINARS & WORKSHOPS
- Starting & Succeeding with Your Small Business
- You Need a Business Plan!
- Recordkeeping for Small Business
- Marketing Your Business
- Techniques of Self Publishing

TEXTBOOKS
"Out of Your Mind... and Into the Marketplace™"
- Step-By-Step Startup
- Copyright, Trademarks, Patents
- DBAs & Resale Tax Numbers
- Recordkeeping, Financing
- Marketing & Advertising

"Anatomy of a Business Plan"
- Preparation Instruction
- Easy-To-Follow Format
- Information Resources
- Examples & Forms

CASSETTE PROGRAMS
- Starting & Succeeding with Your Small Business
- Create Your Business Plan!

Jerry Jinnett   Linda Pinson

- **SMALL BUSINESS OWNERS**
  — over 25 years' experience in the wholesale, retail & service industries.
- **AUTHORS**
  — business textbooks written in step-by-step format for aspiring entrepreneurs.
- **CONSULTANTS**
- **SEMINAR & WORKSHOP INSTRUCTORS**
  — private, colleges, conferences.
- **SPEAKERS**
  — educational & motivational.

Note: It is important that the reply card is positioned properly.

Presenting Your Business   17

BROCHURE SAMPLE

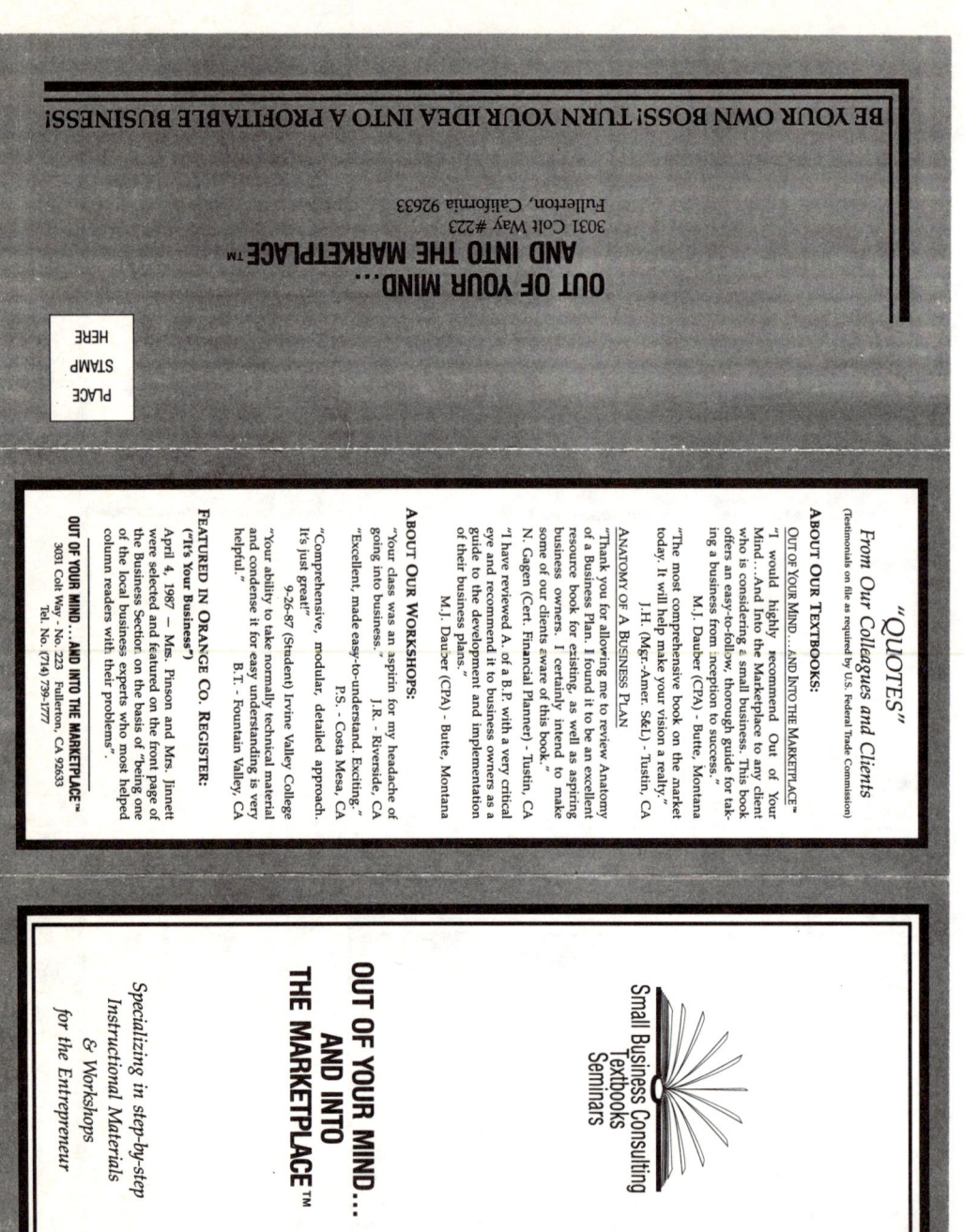

Note: This is a tri-fold brochure. Note the back side for positioning of sections.

18

OUT OF YOUR MIND AND INTO THE MARKETPLACE

MEDIA FLYER SAMPLE
(See Reverse On Next Page)

HOME-BASED BUSINESS

Ten Million U.S. Home-Based Businesses Will Grow to Thirty Million by 1990!

Why the Entrepreneurial Boom?

OUT OF YOUR MIND...AND INTO THE MARKETPLACE ™

is a small-business consulting firm whose purpose is to provide the aspiring entrepreneur with the information necessary to turn an idea into a successful and marketable business.

- Modern technology has made it possible for almost any family to start its own business at home.
- Parents are seeking work that will allow them to stay at home with their families.
- It is more economical to work at home than to rent or buy work space elsewhere.
- Home-based business is a way to avoid difficult and costly commuting.
- The handicapped are discovering working possibilities that enable them to stay at home.
- Job insecurities have forced white-collar workers to pile out of corporations.
- Factory shutdowns from 1979 to 1984 caused 11 1/2 million Americans to lose their jobs. Only 60% have found other work.
- Above all - PEOPLE WANT TO WORK FOR THEMSELVES!

Jerry Jinnett   Linda Pinson

- **HOME-BASED BUSINESS OWNERS**
  — over 25 year's experience in the wholesale, retail & service industries.
- **AUTHORS**
  — business textbooks written in step-by-step format for aspiring entrepreneurs.
- **CONSULTANTS**
- **SEMINAR & WORKSHOP INSTRUCTORS**
  — private, colleges, conferences.
- **SPEAKERS**
  — educational & motivational.

Your listeners will stay tuned . . .

— **We are informative:** We can answer questions in layman's language and guide the listener through all phases of home-based business start-up.

— **We are entertaining:** Let us share the "ups and downs" encountered on the road to business success.

— **We are inspirational:** Educated in the "School of Hard Knocks:, we made it. So can your listeners!

FOR FURTHER INFORMATION, CONTACT:

OUT OF YOUR MIND....
AND INTO THE MARKETPLACE ™

Linda Pinson
Jerry Jinnett
3031 Colt Way #223, Fullerton, CA 92633
(714) 739-1777

Presenting Your Business

MEDIA FLYER SAMPLE
(Use Back for Product Promotion)

**Small Business Consulting
Textbooks
Seminars**

OUT OF YOUR MIND...
AND INTO THE MARKETPLACE™

3031 Colt Way, No. 223, Fullerton, CA 92633 (714) 739-1777

L.C. No. 87-91959
ISBN # 0-944205-00-3
Price $28.00

"Out of Your Mind...and Into the Marketplace"™
- Step-By-Step Startup
- Copyright, Trademarks, Patents
- DBA's & Resale Tax Numbers
- Recordkeeping, Financing
- Marketing & Advertising

"I would highly recommend Out of Your Mind...and Into the Marketplace to any client who is considering a small business. This book offers an easy-to-follow, thorough guide for taking a business from inception to success."
M.J. Dauber (CPA) - Butte, MT

"The most comprehensive book on the market today. It will help make your vision a reality."
J.H. (Mgr.-Amer. S&L) - Tustin, CA

"Anatomy of a Business Plan"
- Preparation Instruction
- Easy-To-Follow Format
- Information Resources
- Examples & Forms

"Thank you for allowing me to review Anatomy of a Business Plan. I found it to be an excellent resource book for existing, as well as aspiring business owner. I certainly intend to make some of our clients aware of this book."
N. Gagen (Cert. Financial Planner) - Tustin, CA

"I have reviewed Anatomy of a Business Plan with a very critical eye and recommend it to business owners as a guide to the development and implementation of their business plan."
M.J. Dauber (CPA) - Butte, MT

L.C. No. 87-91257
ISBN # 0-944205-03-8
Price $21.00

FLYER SAMPLE

Learn To Kayak

OCEAN ADVENTURES
A KAYAKING EXPERIENCE

Jim Busse and Glenn Pinson
13381 White Sand Drive
Tustin, CA. 92680
(714)730-1414

Ocean Adventures offers four different classes to educate the student in every aspect of sea kayaking. Our concepts of safety and education take the student with no kayaking experience to complete self-sufficiency in an ocean kayak. Southern California offers some of the most beautiful conditions under which to learn and our classes take advantage of many of the most exciting local beaches as "classrooms". All lessons are taught personally by Jim or Glenn and are conducted with safety and learning enjoyment as the primary concerns. Jim brings to the sport many years of kayaking experience from both coasts of the United States, British Columbia and Mexico, an expert surfing background and a college education in marine biology. Glenn is an experienced paddler with credentials in seamanship from the United States Coast Guard and in ocean rescue from the National Association of Underwater Instructors.

• • •

BASIC PADDLING COURSE
This beginning course teaches the student the fundamentals of sea kayaking and gives him or her the confidence to venture out on their own. All of the basics are taught in this course including a knowledge of paddling gear, assessment of conditions, basic paddling strokes and an introduction to the three-person rescue. The class is held in Newport Bay and is pre-requisite to all other *Ocean Adventures* courses.

ROLLING COURSE
The rolling course teaches a kayaker to right his craft after capsize without having to exit and re-enter the boat. This is a valuable skill to possess, especially in cold water conditions and in "go-for-it" surfing where capsize is common. Again, this course is taught with safety and self-sufficiency in mind.

SURFING COURSE
The beaches of Southern California have long been known to board surfers for their excellent wave conditions and now kayakers are beginning to discover the art of surfing for themselves. Learn from experienced surfers how to take your boat into mild or the most radical waves and come out on top. This course is for anyone who wants to experience real excitement in a kayak.

ADVANCED COURSE
A course specially designed for the kayaker who wishes to become totally self-sufficient and knowledgable in all aspects of sea kayaking. The abundance of material covered in this course requires a full day of both classroom and on water instruction. Subjects ranging from navigation, survival tactics, variable launch and landing sites, deep water rescue practices and touring techniques will be taught. This is an intense and valuable course for the serious kayaker who wants the most out of their kayaking experiences.

• • •

All boats and kayaking equipment are provided by *Ocean Adventures*. A complete course packet with personal equipment recommendations is available for each class. Please phone or write for more information and specific class meeting dates and times. Classes are kept small but private lessons are available and can be arranged with Ocean Adventures. Reservations are required for all classes.

COME JOIN US ON THE WATER!

BUSINESS CARD SAMPLES

Presenting Your Business

4. PROTECTING YOUR BUSINESS

4. PROTECTING YOUR BUSINESS

We all have great ideas for new products or services. We usually keep these ideas stashed away in the backs of our minds. We think they are silly or we are afraid that if we do disclose them, the idea will be stolen. Don't worry about "silly". Remember the Pet Rock! And where would the sewing machine be if the inventor had decided that putting the eye in the point of the needle was silly? Don't let the fear of having your idea stolen keep you from the marketplace. In order to develop and sell ideas, you have to disclose them.

DISCLOSURE LETTER

One way to protect your idea is through the use of a disclosure letter. This is a letter outlining your idea, detailing the work that has been done to date, and containing sketches, if appropriate. The letter must be dated and notarized. The purpose of the disclosure letter is to verify the date on which the idea was indeed yours. Put the letter in a safe place.

JOURNAL

Establishing a date by means of a disclosure letter is not enough. You must show that you are involved in an **active** business, as opposed to a **passive** business activity. An active business demonstrates continued work and progress in developing the idea into a viable product or service. This may be done by keeping a **log** or **journal.** This is essentially a diary which will show daily entries verifying ongoing work in the business. To be considered a legal document, the log must be a bound book (not loose-leaf), have consecutively numbered pages, be written in ink, and contain no erasures. If mistakes are made, line through the error and make the correction. Make entries listing the people to whom you have spoken about your idea and the dates when the conversations took place. The disclosure letter and the journal will give you the security you need to get your idea "out of your mind".

When you are developing your product, you want to make sure that you are not infringing upon the rights of others. You also want to get protection for your own work. This can be accomplished through the federal laws dealing with copyright, trademark, and patent. Your understanding of the differences in these areas may be helped by the following example. You can **copyright** the artwork on a bag of potato chips, the name and style of type in the logo or mark is **trademarked,** and the recipe or formula for the chips can be **patented.**

COPYRIGHT

The copyright law grants protection to authors of literary, dramatic, musical, and artistic works. The owner of a copyright is granted sole rights to print and reprint, sell and distribute, revise, record, and perform that work. A copyright can only be claimed by the author or those drawing their rights through him. Work created after January 1, 1978 is protected for the life of the author plus 50 years after his death. Three steps should be taken to secure a copyright:

1. **Produce the work with a copyright notice** - the rights to a work will be permanently lost unless **all** copies bear the copyright notice in the required form position. The notice must be securely affixed to the work where it can easily be seen.

2. **Publish the work** - In most cases, you cannot file for a copyright until you have shown or sold at least one item to the public.

3. **Register your claim with the Copyright Office** - As soon as possible, after publication, you must send the following material to the Copyright Office:

> a. **Application for Registration** - The appropriate form can be requested from the Copyright Office. You do not need professional help in filling out the form. It is very straight-forward.
>
> b. **Copies** - Send two copies of the best edition of the work as published. The "best edition" criteria is spelled out in the Copyright Office brochure dealing with your product's classification.
>
> c. **Fee** - The registration fee for published works is $10.00.

Send the registration form, two copies, and the fee in the same envelope or package to the Registrar of Copyrights. Copyright registration becomes effective on the date of receipt in the Copyright Office if all the required elements are in acceptable form.

The **copyright notice** must follow a set format. To arrange the notice in any other manner could make it invalid. As a general rule, the copyright notice should consist of the following three elements:

1. The word **Copyright,** the abbreviation **Copr.,** or the symbol ©.

2. The **year date** of publication - This is ordinarily the year in which copies are first placed on sale.

3. The **name** of the copyright owner or owners.

The three elements described above must appear together on all copies of the work in the following form: © **1987 John Doe.**

There are five classifications for original registration for copyright. The application forms are as follows:

1. **Form TX:** This form covers published and unpublished non-dramatic literary works.

2. **Form SE:** This form is used for serials, works issued or intended to be issued in successive parts bearing numerical or chronological designations and intended to be continued indefinitely, such as periodicals, newspapers, magazines, newsletters, annuals, and journals.

3. **Form PA:** This is the registration form for published and unpublished works of the performing arts (musical and dramatic works, pantomimes and choreographic works, motion pictures and other audiovisual works).

4. **Form VA:** This form is used for published and unpublished works of the visual arts (pictorial, graphic, and sculptural works).

5. **Form SR:** This form is for published and unpublished sound recordings.

Your work may not fit into any of the categories. That does not mean that you cannot secure a copyright. You may also feel that your product falls into more than one category. For clarification, contact the Copyright Office. The address is listed at the end of this section.

TRADEMARK

A trademark is a word, name, symbol, or device, or any combination thereof, used in connection with merchandise and pointing distinctly to the origin or ownership of the article to which it is applied. The strongest trademarks are the least complex. You want your customers to become familiar with your trademark. If your products or services are excellent, your customer will recognize your mark and continue to deal with you. You cannot trademark phrases or names which are in the public domain. Your mark must be unique. When you have decided on a mark, do some research to see that no one else is using it. Then apply it to your goods. A trademark is established through use. You cannot apply for a federal trademark until your mark has been used in interstate trade at least once.

Applications and filing information are available from the Patent and Trademark Office in Washington, D.C. Three steps must be followed to file:

1. **Application for Trademark** - As with the copyright form, the trademark registration form is relatively easy to complete.

2. **Fee** - The registration fee for filing for a trademark is $200.00.

3. **Copies** - Send five specimens showing the mark as it is actually used. If the specimens are three-dimensional, photographs may be used.

There is a standard format for the use of the trademark symbols. The letters ™ should be placed after **every** use of the trademark or symbol. This indicates that you have claimed that mark. Once you have received confirmation from the Trademark Office that your mark has been accepted, you replace ™ with the symbol ®. You may also use: **Registered in U.S. Patent and Trademark Office** or **Reg. U.S. Pat. and Tm. Off.** The following are examples of trademark forms:

New Product ™
New Product ®
New Product   Registered in U.S. Patent and Trademark Office
New Product Reg. U.S. Pat. and Tm. Office

It may take several months for your application to be processed. Once qualified, the mark can be used for twenty years. It may be renewed after that time.

PATENTS

A patent grants an exclusive property right to an invention. It is issued by the Commissioner of Patents and Trademarks within the U.S. Department of Commerce. It gives an inventor the right to exclude others from making, using, or selling an invention for a period of seventeen years. A patent can only be renewed by an act of Congress.

Professional assistance in securing a patent is strongly recommended because patent procedures are quite lengthy and detailed.

When you get an idea for a new invention or process, write down your idea. Analyze the idea for originality and patentability.

One of the most crucial and difficult steps on the way to securing a patent is the determination of **novelty**. Establishing novelty involves two things:

1. **Analyzing the device according to specific standards set down by the Trademark Office.**
2. **Seeing whether or not anyone else has patented it first.**

The only sure way to do this is to conduct a search of the Patent Office files. A search of patents can be informative. Beside indicating if your device is patentable, it may disclose patents better than yours, but not in production. With permission of the holder of the patent, these may be profitably manufactured and sold by your company.

The advantages of obtaining a patent are obvious. You must also realize that a number of obstacles may lie in your path. One of these obstacles is **interference**. This occurs when two or more applicants have applications pending for substantially the same invention. Another is **infringement** which occurs through the unauthorized manufacture, use, or sale of a patented item. A patent does not provide immunity from legal action. In fact, it seems to attract challenges to its legality. As one patent lawyer has said, "A patent is merely a fighting interest in a lawsuit."

If you find your invention to be patentable, your next step is the preparation of a patent application. The application should be filled out in the name of the inventor. Application for a patent is made to the Commissioner of Patents and Trademarks and includes:

1. A **written document** comprised of a petition, an oath, and a specification (descriptions and claims).
2. A **drawing** or **model.**
3. A **filing fee.**

It generally takes an average of nineteen months to get a patent.

For your information, the names and addresses of Federal Agencies issuing publications covering the above areas are listed on the next page. You may contact them and request the information cited or ask for their catalogue of publications.

Protecting Your Business

COPYRIGHT, TRADEMARK, PATENT

(Federal Agencies & Publications)

COPYRIGHT OFFICE
Information and Publications Section, LM-455
Library of Congress
Washington, D.C. 20559

    Publications: 1. Catalogue of materials published
                          2. Highlights of the New Copyright Law (#R99)
                          3. Copyright Basics (R1)
                          4. Trademarks (#R13)

PATENT & TRADEMARK OFFICE
U.S. Department of Commerce
Washington, D.C. 20231

    Note: Write and ask for catalogue of publications.

SUPERINTENDENT OF DOCUMENTS
U.S. Government Printing Office
Washington, D.C. 20402

    Write for: 1. General information concerning patents
                      2. General information concerning trademarks

U.S. SMALL BUSINESS ADMINISTRATION
1441 L. Street, N.W.
Washington, D.C. 20616

    Write for: 1. Introduction to Patents #MA 6.005
                      2. New Product Development #90

5. LEGAL STRUCTURES

5. LEGAL STRUCTURES

Before entering the business arena, you must choose the legal structure which will best suit your needs and the needs of your particular business. There are three principal kinds of business structure: the sole proprietorship, the partnership, and the corporation. The advantages and disadvantages of each must be examined in terms of your specific circumstances.

SOLE PROPRIETORSHIP

A sole proprietorship is owned and operated by one person. This is the simplest, least expensive business organization. Many who are just starting a business choose this form until it becomes practical to enter into a partnership or to incorporate. The advantages of a sole proprietorship include:

1. **Ease of formation** - There are fewer legal restrictions associated with forming a sole proprietorship.

2. **Sole owner of the profits** - All profits go to you, the owner, as do the losses!

3. **Least expensive to establish** - Costs vary according to the city in which the business is formed, but usually include a license fee and may include a business tax. This information can be obtained by calling the Business License Bureau of the city government. If you live in an unincorporated area, contact the county offices.

4. **Fewer records needed with a minimum of regulations.**

5. **Taxed as an individual** - As sole owner, your business profit and loss is recorded on Federal Tax Form 1040, Schedule C, and the bottom line amount transferred to your personal tax form. You will also file Schedule SE which is your contribution to Social Security.

Legal Structures

6. **Total Control** - The business is owned and operated by one person. The control and decision making are vested in you as the owner.

The major disadvantages of a sole proprietorship are:

1. **Unlimited personal liability** - You will be responsible for the full amount of business debt which may exceed the investment. This liability extends to all assets such as home and car.

2. **Less available capital** - Funding must come from the proprietor and obtaining long term financing may be difficult. Loans are based on the strengths of the individual.

3. **Limited growth potential** - The future of the company is dependent upon your capabilities in terms of knowledge, drive and financial potential.

4. **Heavy responsibility**-You are the only person responsible for the business.

PARTNERSHIP

A partnership is a legal business relationship in which two or more people agree to share ownership and management of a business. Often a partner is chosen who possesses skills or expertise you may lack. Sharing ownership of a business may be a way to gain more start-up money. Care should be taken when choosing a partner. This is a close working relationship and you must look carefully at the work style, character, personality, financial situation, skill and expertise of your potential partner. Evaluate the advantages and disadvantages of this legal structure as well as the types of partnerships, before making a decision. **The advantages of a partnership include:**

1. **Ease of formation** - The legal requirements and expenses are fewer than those involved with forming a corporation.

2. **Shared responsibility** - By sharing in the profits, partners are motivated to succeed. This form allows for the distribution of the work load and allows for a sharing of ideas, skills and responsibilities.

3. **Increased growth potential** - A partnership makes it possible to obtain more capital and to tap into more skills.

4. **Ease of operation** - More freedom from government control and special taxation than the corporation.

Some disadvantages of a partnership are:

1. **Unlimited personal liability** - Owners are personally responsible for the business debt.

2. **Lack of continuity** - Like the sole proprietorship, the partnership terminates upon the death or the withdrawal of a general partner unless the partnership agreement provides otherwise.

3. **Relative difficulty in obtaining large sums of capital** - While the opportunity for getting long-term financing is greater in a partnership, it is still dependent upon review of the individual partner's assets.

4. **Difficulty in disposing of the partnership interest** - The buying out of a partnership or sale to another party must be spelled out in the partnership agreement.

5. **Distribution of responsibility in bankruptcy** - In case of bankruptcy, the partner with more personal assets will lose more.

6. **Partner's responsibility** - Each general partner can act on behalf of the company in conducting business. Choose someone you trust; you will be bound by each other's decisions.

7. **Profits** - Profits are shared among the partners according to the terms set out in the agreement.

There are different types of partnerships dependent upon how active a role is played in the business. **General** or **active** partners share equally in the responsibility for managing and financing the business. They also share equally in the liability. A **silent** partner does not participate in the running of the business. His contribution is financial or advisory in nature. A **limited** partner risks only his or her investment in the business and is not subject to the same liabilities as a general partner as long as he or she does not participate in the management and control of the enterprise.

PARTNERSHIP AGREEMENTS

Do not underestimate the need for a partnership agreement. Many friendships and good working relationships have ended over business disagreements. When financial considerations enter the picture, friendships are often put aside. Take some time and carefully prepare a partnership agreement and have it notarized. It will serve as the guideline for your working relationship with your partners. It will outline the contributions by the partners into the business (financial, managerial, material) and delineate the roles of the partners in the business relationship.

Following are concerns which should be covered in a partnership agreement:

1. Name, purpose, address of the business.
2. Duration of the agreement
3. Name, address of each partner
4. Character of partners - general, limited, active, or silent.
5. Contributions of partners - Spell out the financial and managerial contributions expected of each partner.
6. Business expenses - How will they be handled? Who pays the bills and writes the checks? Will you require more than one signature on a check? These are some considerations that will be addressed in this section.
7. Authority - Who will make the decisions? Will they be made jointly?
8. Books, records, and methods of accounting - The form your financial recordkeeping will take is noted here.
9. Division of profits and losses.
10. Draws and salaries - Agree and put in writing how money is to be taken out of the company.
11. Rights of the continuing partner. The terms under which one partner may leave the business and the buyout by another partner can be explained in this section.
12. Death of a partner - Arrangements for continuation of the business in the event of the death of a partner should be made. Without such a clause, the business will end with the death of a partner.

A sample copy of a partnership agreement appears at the end of this chapter. Partnership agreement forms may be purchased at any large office supply or stationers.

CORPORATION

The corporation is the most complex of the three business structures. A corporation is a distinct legal entity, separate from the individuals who own it. It is formed by the authority of the State government, with the approval from the Secretary of State. If business is conducted in more than one state, you must comply with the Federal laws regarding interstate commerce. Federal and state laws may vary considerably. Corporations differ so much in size and type that it is hard to generalize.

However, there are several advantages that are common to most corporations:

1. Ownership is readily transferable. The corporation does not cease to exist with the death of an owner.

2. A corporation has access to numerous investors and can raise substantial capital through the sale of stock.

3. Separate legal existence - The corporation, as a separate legal entity, is responsible and liable for all debts. The shareholders are liable only for the amount they have invested.

4. Ability to draw on the expertise and skills of more than one individual. Authority can be delegated.

Some disadvantages of a corporation are:

1. Extensive government regulations and burdensome local, state, and federal reports.

2. Expensive to form

3. Double taxation - Income tax is paid on corporate net income (profit) and on individual salaries and dividends. This double taxation may be avoided in specific instance by electing to form a Subchapter S corporation.

SUBCHAPTER S

Subchapter S status allows the small business corporation to have its income taxed to the shareholders as if the corporation were a partnership. One objective is to overcome the double tax feature of our system of taxing corporate income and stockholder dividends separately. There are specific conditions for making and maintaining a Subchapter S election:

1. The corporation must have ten or fewer shareholders, all of whom are individuals or estates.

2. There are no nonresident alien shareholders.

3. There is only one class of outstanding stock.

4. All shareholders consent to the election of Subchapter S.

5. A specific portion of the corporation's receipts must be derived from active business rather than passive investments.

6. No limit is placed on the size of the corporation's income and assets.

Legal Structures

Because of the complexity of the corporation, you may wish to consult an attorney regarding its formation. Whether you choose to form the corporation on your own or with legal help, you will have to consider the following items in order to be knowledgeable and prepared.

Carefully choose your location. You will obtain a charter from the state in which the greatest part of your business is conducted. Tax laws vary and some states may have a more favorable tax structure for your type of business.

The preparation of a **'certificate of incorporation'** is generally the first step to incorporating. Many states have a standard certificate of incorporation form which may be used in small businesses. Copies may be obtained from the state official who grants charters or from larger stationers or office suppliers. The following information is usually required:

>1. Corporate name of company - The name chosen must not be similar to any other corporation authorized to do business in the state. The name must not be deceptive so as to mislead the public. To be certain that the name you select is suitable, check out the availability through the designated State official in each state in which you intend to do business before drawing up the certificate of incorporation. In California, contact:
>
>>Office of Name Availability
>>Secretary of State
>>1230 J. Street, Room 100
>>Sacramento, CA 95814
>
>A preliminary check of two names at no charge can be made by phoning (916) 322-2387. You can ask for further information regarding reservation and registration of a corporate name.
>
>2. Purposes for which the corporation is formed - Purposes should be broad enough to allow for expansion and specific enough to give a clear idea of the business to be performed. Reference books and certificates of existing corporations are available at your local library and can provide examples of such clauses.
>
>3. Length of time for which the corporation will exist - The term may cover a number of years or be "perpetual".

4. Names and addresses of incorporators - In some areas, at least one or more of the incorporators is required to be a resident of the state in which the corporation is being organized.

5. Location of the registered office of the corporation in the state of incorporation - If you decide to obtain your charter from another state, you will be required to have an office there. You may appoint an agent in that state to act for you. The agent will be required only to represent the corporation, to maintain a duplicate list of stockholders, and to receive and reply to suits brought against the corporation in the state of incorporation.

6. Proposed capital structure - State maximum amount and type of capital stock which your corporation wishes authorization to issue.

7. The amount of capital required at the time of incorporation.

8. The provisions for the regulation of the internal affairs of the corporation.

9. The name and address of the person who will serve as the director until the first meeting of the stockholders.

The charter will be issued when and if the designated state official determines that the name is available, that the certificate has been completely and properly executed, and that there has been no violation of state law.

In order to complete the incorporation process, the stockholders must meet. They must hold an election of a board of directors and adopt by-laws. The board of directors will in turn elect the officers who will actually have charge of the operation of the corporation. Usually, the officers include president, secretary and treasurer. In small corporations, the members of the board of directors are frequently elected as officers of the corporation.

The by-laws of the corporation may repeat some of the provisions of the charter and usually cover such items as the following:

1. Location of principal office and other offices.
2. Time, place, and notice of stockholder meetings.
3. Number of directors, their compensation, term of office, method of election, and the filling of vacancies.
4. Time and place of director's meetings.
5. Quorum and voting methods.

Legal Structures

6. Methods of selecting officers, titles, duties, terms of office, and salaries.
7. Insurance and form of stock certificates.
8. Method of paying dividends.
9. Decisions regarding the fiscal year.
10. Procedure for amending the by-laws.

Give careful consideration to the three types of legal structure, and base your decision upon a personal evaluation of the following items:

1. The size of risk - Look at the amount of the owner's liability for debts and taxes under each structure.
2. Continuity of the business if something should unexpectedly happen to the owner.
3. The start-up procedure and costs and your ability to attract capital.
4. Be objective regarding your experience and abilities and your own personal financial situation.
5. Project your ultimate goal and purpose for your business and see which legal structure best serves that purpose.
6. Evaluate the possibilities for business growth.

SUMMARY

Don't be overwhelmed by all the preceding information! It's intended to help you make a knowledgeable decision regarding the legal structure of your business. You may start as a sole proprietorship and later form a partnership as your needs change. You may decide that your needs are best served by starting as a corporation. If you change the structure of an existing business, you must notify the governing entities and file the appropriate forms to effect the change. Consult a lawyer if you need help in determining the best type of organization for you. You may find help from the following resources:

Available from library or bookstore:

1. "The Partnership Book: How to Write your Own Partnership Agreement", Clifford, Denis and Ralph Warner, Nolo Press, Berkeley, 1984.

2. "How to Form your own California Corporation", Mancuso, Anthony, Nolo Press, Berkeley, 1985.

Or you may write to:

> Small Business Administration
> P.O. Box 15434
> Fort Worth, TX 76119

Request the following publications for which there may be a charge:

1. Management Aid #6.004: "Selecting the Legal Structure of Your Firm".
2. Management Aid #6.003: "Incorporating a Small Business".

SAMPLE PARTNERSHIP AGREEMENT

PARTNERSHIP AGREEMENT

This partnership agreement is entered into this _____ day of _____, 19___, between the following persons whose names and addresses are set forth below:

The above partners hereby agree that upon the commencement date of this partnership, they shall be deemed to have become partners in business. The purposes, terms, and conditions of this partnership are as follows:

    1. **NAME** - The firm name of the partnership shall be

    2. **PRINCIPAL PLACE OF BUSINESS** - The principal place of business of the partnership shall be

    3. **PURPOSE** - The business of the partnership is set forth below and includes any other business related thereto.

    4. **TERM** - The partnership shall commence on _____, 19___, and shall continue until_____.

Legal Structures

SAMPLE PARTNERSHIP AGREEMENT - page 2

5. CAPITAL CONTRIBUTION: DISTRIBUTION OF PROFITS AND LOSSES

Name of Partner	Capital Contribution		Percentage Distribution of Profit & Loss
	Specific Contribution	Agreed Cash Valuation of Contribution	

A division of profits and losses shall be made at such time as may be agreed upon by the partners and at the close of each fiscal year. The profits and losses of the partnership shall be divided between the partners according to the above Schedule of "Distribution of Profits and Losses".

6. CONTROL- The partners shall have the exclusive control over the business of the partnership and each partner shall have equal rights in the management conduct of the partnership business. Any differences arising as to the ordinary matters connected with the partnership business shall be decided by a numerical majority of the partners. Any act beyond the scope of this partnership agreement or any contract which may subject this partnership to liability in excess of _____ DOLLARS shall be subject to the prior written consent of all the partners.

SAMPLE PARTNERSHIP AGREEMENT – page 3

IN WITNESS WHEREOF, the parties hereto have signed this partnership agreement on the day and year first written above.

_____
PARTNER

_____
PARTNER

_____
PARTNER

_____
PARTNER

Legal Structures

6.
SECURING A BUSINESS LICENSE

6. SECURING A BUSINESS LICENSE

BUSINESS LICENSE

If your business is going to operate within the law, it will be necessary for you to obtain a license or permit in the city or country in which you will be doing business. If that business is service-related and performs any portion of its work in other cities outside of it's operational center you may also be required to buy licenses in those cities. For example, if you have a repair service and you make several calls to homes away from the city where your shop is located, you could be obligated to purchase licenses in the cities you service. It is true that many businesses are operating without licenses. However, a business license is inexpensive and lends credibility to your operation. Without one, you run the risk of being discovered and barred from doing business at all. A fine may also be imposed. Business licenses are serious matters in most cities, and provide them with a source of revenue and a means of controlling the types of businesses that operate within their jurisdictions.

SELECTING A LOCATION

In most instances, your first contact should be the City or County Clerk's Office in the city where you wish to locate your base of operation. They are an excellent source of information regarding police, fire and health permits needed for your business. If you have elected to have a home-based business, restrictions may not permit you to operate in your city. You may be forced to move your business outside the home or operated outside of the law. If your family happens to be moving, and you are a seasoned entrepreneur, you may wish to select your home partly on the basis of whether or not that city's ordinances will allow you to operate a home-based business.

Securing a Business License

Different types of businesses may be subject to special restrictions. For instance, a mail-order business may be allowed in your home, while a direct-sales operation may not be. Repair services may be allowed, but only if they do not involve the use of toxic chemicals. Food services may be disallowed, but the city may allow you to use your home as an administrative office for your business. Generally speaking, home-based businesses are not permitted to change the appearance of the neighborhood and, therefore, you may be prohibited to use advertising or equipment that can be viewed from the street. Very often, police or fire inspections will be conducted to see that your business does not violate any of several restrictions. Ground work in this area may save you a lot of problems down the road.

Any business location must fall within the zoning regulations. You may obtain zoning verification from the zoning commission to determine if your business is approved for the location you have chosen. Home-based businesses may wish to refer to the NAHB Model Zoning Ordinance.

BUSINESS LICENSE APPLICATION

Once you have determined that your business meets all the specific requirements for operation within the city you have chose, you are ready for a trip to the Business License Bureau or the City or the County Clerk's Office to legalize your business. You will be asked to fill out an application. You will be required to supply such specifics as name, address of business, type of business, number of employees, expected gross, vehicles to be operated, and any other information which may be relevant. You will probably have to leave your completed application, along with a fee. Your application will be reviewed and a license will either be issued or refused within a few days. It is then renewed annually, subject to adherence to that city's codes and regulations.

7.

REGISTERING A FICTITIOUS NAME (DBA)

7. REGISTERING A FICTITIOUS NAME (DBA)

DBA

If you plan to conduct your business under a fictitious name then you must file a DBA, which stands for "**DOING BUSINESS AS**". A fictitious name is any business name that does not contain your own name as a part of it. In some states, that means your legal name.

Examples are as follows:

1. Ocean Adventures - DBA required
2. Glenn's Ocean Adventures - DBA required
3. Smith's Ocean Adventures - DBA may be required
4. Glenn Smith's Ocean Adventures - No DBA required

It has been discussed in a previous chapter titled **Choosing a Business Name** that your business name should be free of conflict with names already registered. Please refer back for information.

PUBLISHING YOUR FICTITIOUS NAME

Assuming that you have chosen a fictitious name, it is time to register it — or file it with the city or county in which you are doing business. The first step is to place a legal ad in a general circulation newspaper. This is done following the securing of a business license. That newspaper's circulation must be in the county in which you conduct your business. Usually, the ad must run in four consecutive issues. Its purpose is to inform the general public that you are beginning operation under your assumed name and that you are the individual who will be conducting that business.

PUBLICATION CERTIFICATE

When you have published your fictitious name, a Publication Certificate has to be filed with the City or County Clerk. You may do so by going to the appropriate office with proof of publication (the copies from the four newspaper editions). The filing fee generally runs between $10.00 and $25.00. Some newspapers will collect your fees and file for you after publishing. Others publish only and require that you do your own filing. It would be wise for you to do some calling to various newspapers and ask the following questions:

1. What is the charge for the publication of a DBA?
2. Does the newspaper notify the City or County Clerk for you? If so, what are the fees involved?
3. What is the circulation of the newspaper?
4. What information do you need to take to the newspaper?

After determining which newspaper suits your purpose best, you are ready for a trip to their office to publish your statement and file your Publication Certificate with the City or County Clerk. The fees may vary greatly, but usually run between $40.00 and $100.00 for publication. When your fictitious name is published, you will be sent a copy of the publication. If the newspaper is going to file for you with the City or County Clerk, they will also send you proof that it has been recorded.

RENEWALS

You will be required to renew your DBA at certain intervals — such as every five years. You will be notified when it is time to renew. However, it is your responsibility to know when it must be done and to protect yourself by doing so. Renewal does not require republishing, but will probably involve a fee to the City or County Clerk.

BENEFITS OF OWNERSHIP

Registering a business name is very important for your own protection as well as for compliance with the law. Registration of that name gives you exclusive rights to it and keeps others from filing the same or a similar name and capitalizing on the hard work and investments made by you in your business. The time and money spent is very small compared to the benefits you will derive from becoming the owner of your business name.

FICTITIOUS BUSINESS NAME STATEMENT
SAMPLE FORM

SEE REVERSE SIDE FOR INSTRUCTIONS — **NOT VALID UNLESS CLERK'S ENDORSEMENT APPEARS BELOW**

LEE A. BRANCH
COUNTY CLERK
700 CIVIC CENTER DRIVE, WEST
P.O. BOX 838
SANTA ANA, CALIFORNIA 92702

NOTICE - THIS FICTITIOUS STATEMENT EXPIRES ON DECEMBER 31, 1991

FILED JAN 6 - 1986   County Clerk
By _____ Deputy

A NEW STATEMENT MUST BE FILED PRIOR TO DECEMBER 31, 1991

REMINDER
1. Submit original and 3 copies.
2. Filing fee $10.00 for one business name, $2.00 for each additional business name, $2.00 for each additional partner after first two.
3. Provide return stamped envelope, if mailed.

FICTITIOUS BUSINESS NAME STATEMENT

This statement was filed with the County Clerk of Orange County on date indicated by file stamp above.

THE FOLLOWING PERSON(S) IS(ARE) DOING BUSINESS AS: (TYPE ALL INFORMATION)

1. Fictitious Business Name(s)

2. Street Address, City & State of Principal place of Business in California   Zip Code

3. Full name of Registrant   (If corporation—show state of Incorporation)

   Residence Address   City   State   Zip Code

   Full name of Registrant   (If corporation—show state of Incorporation)

   Residence Address   City   State   Zip Code

   Full name of Registrant   (If corporation—show state of Incorporation)

   Residence Address   City   State   Zip Code

   Full name of Registrant   (If corporation—show state of Incorporation)

   Residence Address   City   State   Zip Code

4. (CHECK ONE ONLY) This business is conducted by ( ) an individual (X) a general partnership ( ) a limited partnership ( ) an unincorporated association other than a partnership ( ) a corporation ( ) a business trust ( ) co-partners ( ) husband and wife ( ) joint venture ( ) other—please specify _____

5. Signed _____
   (TYPE OR PRINT NAME)

   If Registrant a corporation sign below:
   Corporation Name _____
   Signature & Title _____
   (TYPE OR PRINT NAME AND TITLE)

[ ] New Fictitious Business Name Statement
[ ] Refile

CERTIFICATION
I hereby certify that the foregoing is a correct copy of the original on file in my office.
Lee A. Branch, County Clerk
By _____ Deputy

File No. _____   FILE NO. F297553

REGISTRANT'S COPY

Registering a Fictitious Name (DBA)

PUBLICATION CERTIFICATE SAMPLE

PROOF OF PUBLICATION
(2015.5 C.C.P.)

STATE OF CALIFORNIA
COUNTY OF ORANGE

I am a citizen of the United States and a resident of the County aforesaid; I am over the age of eighteen years, and not a party to or interested in the above-entitled matter. I am the principal clerk of the printer of the Orange City News, a newspaper of general circulation, printed and published weekly in the City of Orange, County of Orange, and which newspaper has been adjudged a newspaper of general circulation by the Superior Court of the County of Orange, State of California, under the date of August 17, 1970, Case Number A-66522, that the notice of which the annexed is a printed copy (set in type not smaller than nonpareil), has been published in each regular and entire issue of said newspaper and not in any supplement thereof on the following dates, to-wit:

...... 1/15, 1/22, 1/29, 2/5 ......

all in the year 19..86..

I certify (or declare) under penalty of perjury that the foregoing is true and correct.

Dated at Orange, California, this ....5th.... day
of ..February.............., 19..86..

....
Signature

ORANGE CITY NEWS
533 W Collins
Orange, California 92668

OCN FORM NO. 0023-6/78-52118-2M

This space is for the County Clerk's Filing Stamp

FILED
FEB 5 1986
GARY L. GRANVILLE, County Clerk
By................ DEPUTY

Proof of Publication of

FICTITIOUS BUSINESS NAME STATEMENT.
The following persons are doing business as: BUNZ, 13381 White Sand Dr., Tustin, CA 92680.
Linda J. Pinson, 13381 White Sand Dr., Tustin, CA 92680.
Jerry A. Jinnett, 3031 Colt Way, No. 223, Fullerton, CA 92633.
This business is conducted by a general partnership.
Signed: Linda J. Pinson.
This statement was filed with the County Clerk of Orange County on January 8, 1986.
File No. F297553
Pub. Orange City News January 15, 22, 29, February 5, 1986.
OCN 160

PROOF OF PUBLICATION

8. HOME-BASED BUSINESS

8. HOME-BASED BUSINESS

If you are going into business, there is a very good chance that you are planning on a **home-based business.** The trend in that direction has developed out of a necessity to reduce overhead and, in many cases, to allow working parents the opportunity to earn income without leaving their homes. Home-based businesses can be very successful. However, without certain considerations, they can turn into disasters or, at the very least, unproductive semi-attempts at dabbling in business.

SELF DISCIPLINE

It is a fact that owning one's own business requires a great deal of time and effort. Working for yourself is equivalent to holding down two jobs. For this reason, it will be necessary to develop a high degree of self-discipline. Be willing to work long hours and do not put off the tasks that need to be done. Decide what hours you want to work and stick to your schedule. Don't fall into the trap of thinking you are free. You are your own boss and you will have to treat yourself as you would an employee.

WORK SPACE

Set aside a space that will be used for your business. Organize your work space in an efficient manner and eliminate non-work items so that you will not be tempted to mix the two during working hours. Also keep in mind that to be tax deductible, that area must be used exclusively for your business.

INTERRUPTIONS

Inform your family and friends that you are serious about your business and will need to be able to work without interruption. There have been many times when we have worked late into the night because well-meaning friends decided we needed their company over coffee during the day. This is one of the most serious problems encountered in home-based businesses and one that is difficult to solve.

BUSINESS HOURS

You will need to establish regular business hours. Credibility is hard to come by when you work in your home. Customers will take you more seriously if they see that you are operating on a schedule. If you are out when they call, you will soon find that they will be looking elsewhere for the same service or product.

BE PRESENTABLE

Just because you are working at home, don't feel free to be a slob. A home-based business is the perfect target for a 24-hour a day onslaught by your customers. They will ring your door bell seven days a week from dawn to dark. If you are going to answer it, look like a business person. If your customer is going to have confidence in your service, he must first have confidence in you.

PROTECT YOUR FREE HOURS

You will have little time to spare if your business is going to prosper. You will have to plan for free time. Decide what days you wish to be closed and use them for non-business pursuits. Be sure to inform your customers in regard to your working hours and tell them you are closed if they want to come during your off hours. Most will respect you and return during business hours.

PROFESSIONALISM

Above all, conduct your business in a professional manner. Home-based businesses are often regarded as "little hobbies". I wish I had a nickel for every time I have heard the statement made about what a wonderful hobby the clock business is. Obviously, we are in business for reasons other than having fun.

HOME-BASED BUSINESS represent a large segment of today's economy. Keep in mind that yours can prosper, but only if you run it like a business. Make it work for you and you will be the proud owner of a successful, rewarding and respected home-based business!!!

9. OBTAINING A SELLER'S PERMIT

9. OBTAINING A SELLER'S PERMIT

Anyone who purchases items for resale or who provides a taxable service must obtain a **seller's permit number**. This number is required in all states where sales tax is collected.

APPLICATION

A seller's permit is obtained through the State Board of Equalization. An application from the California State Board of Equalization is included as a sample for your information. After filling out your application, you will be called in to interview. Following this interview and a review of your application, it will be determined whether or not you qualify for a Seller's permit. For this reason, it is imperative that you understand exactly what you are requesting and the purpose for which you are requesting it. The wrong answer to a question can result in a denial of a certificate.

PURPOSE OF A SELLER'S PERMIT

A sales tax is imposed upon retailers for the privilege of selling tangible personal property at retail within a state. The retailer, not the customer, is the person liable and responsible for paying the sales tax. Consequently, every seller engaged in the business of selling a tangible product or of providing a taxable service in a state where sales tax is collected is required to hold a seller's permit for the purpose of reporting and paying their sales and use tax liability. The seller's permit is more commonly referred to as a **resale number.**

Your request must be on the basis that you will be purchasing taxable items for resale and that you will be reselling them either for resale or to the ultimate user or that you will be providing a taxable service. Any other reason for your request will be grounds for denial. For example, many food services are not taxable unless they are provided at an event that charges admission. Therefore, a resale tax number would not be warranted. You may request information sheets from the State Board of Equalization on the sales tax regulations on your particular type of business.

MISUSE

Once you have been issued a resale tax number, it is imperative that you use it only for the purpose for which it was intended. The penalties for misuse are very serious and may involve a heavy fine and/or a jail sentence. Many tax numbers have been used to avoid paying sales tax on business-related purchases as well as tax on personal items. The rule of thumb is: If you do not intend to resell your purchase through your business, do not use your resale number to buy it tax free. At this point, let us say that there is some validity to using your resale number to purchase wholesale. Many wholesalers do ask you to file a resale card with them before selling to you at wholesale prices. This does not mean you do not pay sales tax if you are not purchasing for resale. It may only be a means of adding credibility as a business owner.

RESALE CERTIFICATE

If you are purchasing goods for resale, the supplier or manufacturer will ask you to fill out a resale certificate which he must keep on file to validate his selling to you on a tax-free basis. By the same token, when you sell to another dealer, you must also have him fill out a resale card for your files. If the state later questions your nontaxable sales, you will have documentation as to why you did not collect tax on a sale. Pads of resale certificates may be purchased at almost any stationary supply store. An example is included at the end of this text.

REPORTING SALES TAX

As previously stated, the purpose of a seller's permit is to provide the State with a means of collecting sales tax. To accomplish this, the sales tax must be accounted for by the final seller and sent to the State along with a report of the sources of those taxes. For this reason, the seller must keep accurate records as to the types of sales made and the amount of sales falling within each of the following categories.
1. Gross Sales.
2. Purchase price of property purchased without sales tax and used for purposes other than resale.
3. Sales to other retailers for purposes of resale.
4. Non-taxable labor (repair and installation).
5. Sales to the U.S. Government.
6. Sales in interstate or foreign commerce to out-of-state consumers.
7. Other exempt transactions.

The State may require you to file a report with them either quarterly or annually, probably in accordance with the amount of your gross sales. This report form will be sent to you by the State Board of Equalization. You must complete the report and mail it to the State, along with your check in the amount of sales tax collected, by a certain date (usually January 31st). An example of a **California Sales and Use Tax Return** is included in this chapter for your convenience. When you receive this report, you will also receive a Tax Information Sheet with featured articles on sales tax regulations and crackdowns. Read it carefully. Failure to properly report may result in loss of your resale privilege as well as the more serious penalties mentioned above.

In the event that you are somewhat confused as the progression of goods from the manufacturer to the consumer and final payment of taxes to the State by the seller, we have prepared a **Sales Tax Flow Chart** for you to examine in the hope that it will clarify the above.

APPLICATION SAMPLE
STATE BOARD OF EQUALIZATION

| COMPLETE Front and Back to Apply for a Permit for Part-Time or Full-Time Business. | This is not an Application RETURN IN PERSON |

1. a. Name of Owner _____ Seller's Permit # _____

   b. Name of Corp _____

   c. List Self, Partners or Corporate Officers below:

NAME	HOME ADDRESS, TOWN & ZIP	HOME TELEPHONE	DRIVER'S LICENSE #	SOCIAL SECURITY #
(A)				
(B)				
(C)				
(D)				

2. Fictitious Name/DBA _____ Business Telephone _____

3. Physical Location of your Business _____
   STREET / CITY / ZIP

4. Mailing Address _____
   STREET / CITY / ZIP

5. Purchase Price of Business $ _____ Value of Stock $ _____ Value Equipment $ _____

6. Name/Address of Former Owner? _____

7. Describe Briefly Type of Business and Products Sold _____

8. Date of First Sale _____ Part Time? _____ How Many Employees for Withholding Tax? _____

9. Real Estate Owned (Business/Personal) _____

   a. Value $ _____ Balance Owing $ _____ Payment to Whom? _____ And Town? _____

10. Name/Address of your Landlord at:

    a. Business Location _____

    b. Residence Location _____

11. Estimated Monthly Expenses:

		Estimated Monthly Sales:	
Rent	$ _____	Monthly Gross Average	$ _____
Payroll	$ _____	Non-Taxable Sales	$ _____
Other Expenses	$ _____	Taxable Sales	$ _____
Total	$ _____	Monthly Tax	$ _____

Sales figures are tentatively accepted in setting security requirements. Your file may be reviewed at a later date and the security requirement adjusted accordingly. Taxpayer's initials _____. (OVER)

BOARD USE ONLY: Reporting Basis _____ Security $ _____ Approved _____ Date _____

BT-921 FRONT (8-83)

Obtaining a Seller's Permit

APPLICATION SAMPLE – page 2
STATE BOARD OF EQUALIZATION

12. Major Suppliers and Addresses _____
_____

13. Person to Contact on Business from 8 to 5 _____ 8 to 5 Telephone _____

14. Present or Previous Employer _____
　　　　　　　　　　　　　　　　　　　NAME　　　　　　　ADDRESS　　　　　TOWN

15. Name of Spouse(s) _____ Employer(s) _____
　　　　　　　　　　　　　　　　　　　　　　　　　　　　　　　　　TOWN

16. Accountant/Bookkeeper _____
　　　　　　　　　　　　　NAME　　　　ADDRESS/TOWN　　　TELEPHONE

17. Where Do You Bank (Business and Personal)

　　Checking/Savings _____
　　　　　　　　　　　NAME　　　　　ADDRESS　　　　　TOWN

　　Checking/Savings _____
　　　　　　　　　　　NAME　　　　　ADDRESS　　　　　TOWN

　　Checking/Savings _____
　　　　　　　　　　　NAME　　　　　ADDRESS　　　　　TOWN

　　Credit Union _____
　　　　　　　　　NAME　　　　　ADDRESS　　　　　TOWN

18. Personal References: (Family or Friends)

　　1. _____
　　　　NAME　　　　　ADDRESS/TOWN　　　　　TELEPHONE

　　2. _____
　　　　NAME　　　　　ADDRESS/TOWN　　　　　TELEPHONE

19. FOR USER OF FUEL PERMIT – Motor Vehicles for which Permit is Required. Attach schedule if necessary (Indicate Type of Fuel in Column 4: D for Diesel; L for LPG; N for Natural Gas)

1 Make & Year of Vehicle	2 Engine No. Serial No. or ID	3 License Number	4 Type of Fuel	5 Name of Registered Owner on Date of Application

20. Name and Address of Legal Owner of Vehicles:

　　A. _____

　　B. _____

21. Estimated Monthly Usage of Diesel, Natural Gas or LPG Fuel used in California: (Gallons or Cubic Feet)

22. Other Info: (i.e. Prior Permits, Parent Corporation) _____
_____

23. Signed _____ Title _____ Date _____

BT-921 BACK (8-83)

OUT OF YOUR MIND AND INTO THE MARKETPLACE

RESALE CERTIFICATE SAMPLE

FIRM NAME _____

I HEREBY CERTIFY,
That I hold valid seller's permit No. _____
issued pursuant to the Sales and Use Tax Law; that I am engaged in the business of selling

_____

that the tangible personal property described herein which I shall purchase from:

_____

will be resold by me in the form of tangible personal property; PROVIDED, however, that in the event any of such property is used for any purpose other than retention, demonstration, or display while holding it for sale in the regular course of business, it is understood that I am required by the Sales and Use Tax Law to report and pay for the tax, measured by the purchase price of such property.

Description of property to be purchased: _____

_____

Dated: _____ 19 _____ _____
                                              Signature

at _____ _____
                                              By and Title

Phone _____ _____
                                              Address

AICO-UTILITY Line Form No. 25-086

Obtaining a Seller's Permit

STATE BOARD OF EQUALIZATION
SAMPLE REPORT

BT-401-AC3 FRONT REV. 9 (1-79)
STATE OF CALIFORNIA
BOARD OF EQUALIZATION – Department of Business Taxes

STATE, LOCAL and DISTRICT SALES and USE TAX RETURN

DUE ON OR BEFORE _____ **FOR** PERIOD ____ YEAR ____

PARTIAL PERIOD

Mail to:
STATE BOARD OF EQUALIZATION
P. O. BOX 1799
SACRAMENTO, CA 95808

BUSINESS CODE | AREA CODE | ACCOUNT NUMBER

NAME

WORK COPY

BUSINESS ADDRESS

Not acceptable as a Return by the
State Board of Equalization

CITY | REPORTING BASIS

STATE SALES AND USE TAX — READ INSTRUCTIONS BEFORE PREPARING

1. TOTAL SALES .... IF YOU INCLUDE TAX CHARGED – SEE LINE 9 .... $
2. ADD—Purchase price of tangible personal property purchased without California sales or use tax and used for some purpose other than resale. ENTER "NONE" IF YOU HAVE NOTHING TO REPORT
3. TOTAL (Line 1 plus Line 2) ENTER "NONE" IF YOU HAVE NOTHING TO REPORT .... $

DEDUCT EXEMPT TRANSACTIONS (See Instructions)
4. Sales to other retailers for purposes of resale .... $
5. Nontaxable Sales of Food Products
6. Nontaxable Labor (Repair and Installation)
7. Sales to the United States Government
8. Sales in interstate or foreign commerce to out-of-state consumer
9. Amount of sales tax (if any) included in Line 1
10. Other exempt transactions (See Instruction 10)
11. TOTAL TRANSACTIONS EXEMPT FROM STATE & COUNTY SALES & USE TAX (Lines 4 thru 10) ....
12. Amount on which STATE & COUNTY Sales and Use Tax applies (Line 3 minus Line 11) .... $
13. AMOUNT OF TAX ..... (4¾% State, ¼% County) (Multiply amount on Line 12 by .05) .... $

UNIFORM LOCAL SALES AND USE TAX

14. Amount on which State Tax applies (Enter amount from Line 12) .... $
15. ADD—Other local tax adjustments (See Instruction 15) ....
16. TOTAL (Line 14 plus Line 15) .... $
17. DEDUCT—Transactions exempt from local tax only (See Instruction 17) ..
18. Amount on which LOCAL Tax applies (Line 16 minus Line 17) .... $
19. AMOUNT OF LOCAL TAX 1% (Multiply amount on Line 18 by .01) .... $

DISTRICT SALES AND USE TAX

20a. Amount of San Francisco Bay Area Rapid Transit District Tax (From Line A12 Column A of Schedule A) .... $
20b. Amount of Santa Clara County Transit District Tax (From Line A12 Column B of Schedule A) .... $
20c. Amount of Santa Cruz Metropolitan Transit District Tax (From Line A12 Column C of Schedule A) .... $

TOTAL TAX

21. TOTAL STATE, COUNTY, LOCAL & DISTRICT TAX (Total of Lines 13, 19, 20a, 20b & 20c) TOTAL TAX $
22. Deduct amount of sales or use tax or reimbursement therefor imposed by other states and paid by you on the purchase of tangible personal property. Purchase price must be included in Line 2. (See Instruction 22)
23. NET STATE, COUNTY, LOCAL AND DISTRICT TAX (Line 21 minus Line 22) ....
24. LESS—Tax Prepayments | 1ST MONTH | 2ND MONTH | Total Prepayments
25. REMAINING STATE, COUNTY, LOCAL AND DISTRICT TAX (Line 23 minus Line 24) .... $
26. Penalty of 10% (.10) if payment is made after the due date shown above .... Penalty
27. Interest of 1% (.01) per month or part of a month if payment is made after above due date ... Interest
28. TOTAL AMOUNT DUE AND PAYABLE (Line 25 plus Lines 26 & 27) .... $

I hereby certify that this return, including any accompanying schedules and statements, has been examined by me and to the best of my knowledge and belief is a true, correct and complete return.

SIGNATURE AND TITLE _____ ( ) _____ PHONE NUMBER

MAKE CHECK OR MONEY ORDER PAYABLE TO STATE BOARD OF EQUALIZATION

Obtaining a Seller's Permit

STATE BOARD OF EQUALIZATION
SAMPLE REPORT FORM - page 2

SCHEDULE A – COMPUTATION SCHEDULE FOR DISTRICT SALES AND USE TAX

PLEASE READ INSTRUCTIONS BEFORE PREPARING THIS SCHEDULE. REVERSE CARBON BEFORE MAKING ENTRIES.

This schedule is to be completed for District Sales and Use Tax on transactions (1) when your business is located in a transit district imposing such taxes and/or (2) you are engaged in business in a transit district and are required to collect the district tax on sales, or leases which are subject to the district use tax.

A1. Amount on which LOCAL Tax applies. (Enter amount from Line 18 on the reverse side) ... $
A2. DEDUCT—Amount of transactions (sales) not subject to district sales or use tax made from locations outside transit district(s) $
A3. Amount of transit district transactions (Line A1 minus Line A2) ... $

ALLOCATE TOTAL ON LINE A3 TO PROPER TRANSIT DISTRICT(S) ON LINE A4	SAN FRANCISCO BAY AREA COLUMN A	DISTRICT SANTA CLARA COUNTY COLUMN B	SANTA CRUZ COUNTY COLUMN C
A4. Enter amount from Line A3 allocated to the proper transit district(s) (Total of this line must equal Line A3 above)	$	$	$
A5. ADD—Other DISTRICT Tax adjustments (See Instruction A5)			
A6. TOTAL—(Line A4 plus Line A5)	$	$	$
DEDUCT EXEMPT TRANSACTIONS (See Instruction A7-9)			
A7. Sales of property shipped to a point outside the district for use elsewhere in California			
A8. Sales made under a fixed price contract or a fixed price lease executed prior to the effective date of the DISTRICT Tax			
A9. Other exempt transactions or adjustments	$	$	$
A10. Total Transactions Exempt from the DISTRICT Tax (Lines A7 through A9)	$	$	$
A11. Amount on which the DISTRICT Tax applies (Line A6 minus Line A10)	$	$	$
A12. Amount of ½% DISTRICT Tax (Multiply amount on Line A11 by .005)	$	$	$
On reverse side, enter amount from Line A12 on:	Line 20a	Line 20b	Line 20c

SCHEDULE B – DETAILED ALLOCATION BY COUNTY OF 1% UNIFORM LOCAL SALES AND USE TAX

PLEASE READ INSTRUCTIONS BEFORE PREPARING THIS SCHEDULE. REVERSE CARBON BEFORE MAKING ENTRIES.

The 1% uniform local sales and use tax on retail sales of merchandise (not involving installation) made at your permanent place of business in California, or local tax on property purchased ex-tax and used at the place of business, should be entered on Line B2 below the county schedule. Enter 1% local tax on all other transactions in Column C of the schedule after the name of the county where the sale or use occurred.

SAMPLE

COUNTY IN WHICH TAXABLE TRANSACTION OCCURRED	CODE	AMOUNT OF 1% LOCAL TAX	COUNTY IN WHICH TAXABLE TRANSACTION OCCURRED	CODE	AMOUNT OF 1% LOCAL TAX	COUNTY IN WHICH TAXABLE TRANSACTION OCCURRED	CODE	AMOUNT OF 1% LOCAL TAX	COUNTY IN WHICH TAXABLE TRANSACTION OCCURRED	CODE	AMOUNT OF 1% LOCAL TAX
ALAMEDA	01		KINGS	16		PLACER	31		SIERRA	46	
ALPINE	02		LAKE	17		PLUMAS	32		SISKIYOU	47	
AMADOR	03		LASSEN	18		RIVERSIDE	33		SOLANO	48	
BUTTE	04		LOS ANGELES	19		SACRAMENTO	34		SONOMA	49	
CALAVERAS	05		MADERA	20		SAN BENITO	35		STANISLAUS	50	
COLUSA	06		MARIN	21		SAN BERNARDINO	36		SUTTER	51	
CONTRA COSTA	07		MARIPOSA	22		SAN DIEGO	37		TEHAMA	52	
DEL NORTE	08		MENDOCINO	23		SAN FRANCISCO	38		TRINITY	53	
EL DORADO	09		MERCED	24		SAN JOAQUIN	39		TULARE	54	
FRESNO	10		MODOC	25		SAN LUIS OBISPO	40		TUOLUMNE	55	
GLENN	11		MONO	26		SAN MATEO	41		VENTURA	56	
HUMBOLDT	12		MONTEREY	27		SANTA BARBARA	42		YOLO	57	
IMPERIAL	13		NAPA	28		SANTA CLARA	43		YUBA	58	
INYO	14		NEVADA	29		SANTA CRUZ	44				
KERN	15		ORANGE	30		SHASTA	45				

B1. Total local tax for all counties listed above ... $
B2. Local tax on sales made and merchandise consumed at your permanent place of business in California. (Do not include any tax allocated to the above counties) [Tax Area Code / Board Use Only]
B3. Total local tax liability (Line B1 plus Line B2) This total must agree with Line 19 on the reverse side ... $

BT-401-AC3 BACK REV. 9 (1-79)

OUT OF YOUR MIND AND INTO THE MARKETPLACE

SALES TAX FLOW CHART

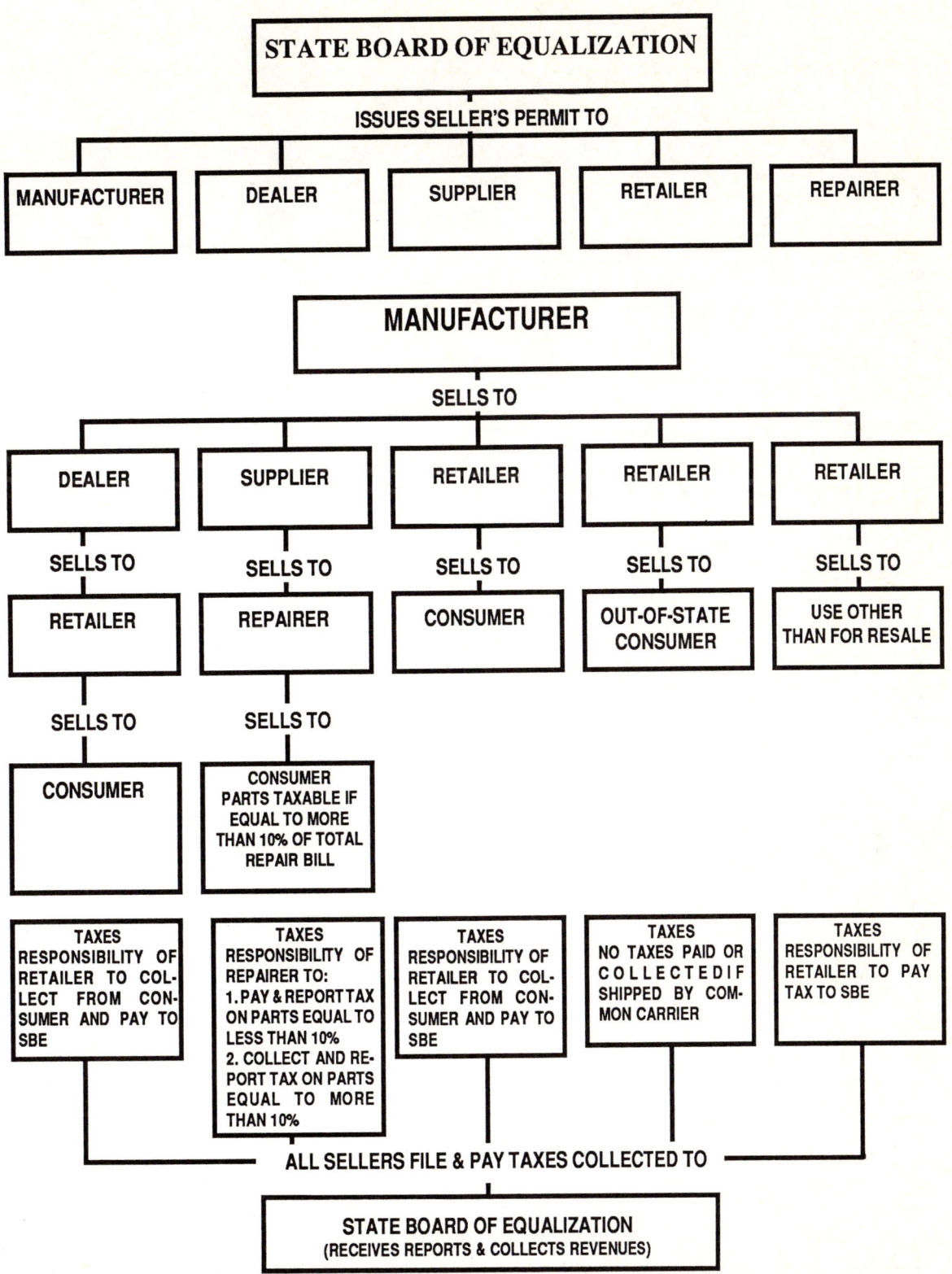

NOTE: When a manufacturer sells to out-of-state retailer who in turn sells to a consumer in that state, the sales tax is collected by the retailer and paid to that state. If mailed directly to consumer, no sales tax is paid.

Obtaining a Seller's Permit

10.

SETTING UP A BANK ACCOUNT

10. SETTING UP A BANK ACCOUNT

CHOOSING A BANK

The selection of the bank with which you will do business should be undertaken with a great deal of consideration. Banks vary greatly in the services they offer, as well as in the charges for those services. You will want to think about such factors as interest rate paid on accounts, locality, hours of operation, loan policies, holding periods, etc. It would be wise for you to spend some time telephoning banks and savings & loan institutions to gather information. At the end of this text, you will find a worksheet (titled **Choosing a Bank**) that will help you to compare advantages and disadvantages of the financial institutions being considered.

SEPARATE BUSINESS & PERSONAL FINANCES

Many times, a new business owner will be tempted to run business finances through personal accounts. **Do not mix** the two. It is imperative that you keep your personal and business finances separate. Failure to do so can only cause you many problems with your recordkeeping and tax computations. Business accounts are necessary for credibility when dealing with other businesses. It may be difficult to establish an open account with a supplier or wholesaler if you do not have a business bank account.

CHECKING ACCOUNT

The first consideration in banking for a small business is generally a checking account. If your business name is an assumed one, you cannot open a checking account under that name without first having filed a DBA as discussed in the previous chapter. It should be noted here, that banking policies at most financial institutions preclude offering interest-bearing checking accounts unless your name is part of the company name. If you have filed a DBA, be sure to take your receipt with you when you open your checking account. The bank will require a copy for their records.

When you open your checking account, you will be asked what style of checks you wish to order. As stipulated in **Recordkeeping,** you will have to decide between the book type and the pocket type. Be sure to think ahead as to your needs. Reordering of checks can be costly. Start with a minimum order in case you want to change later on. At the same time you order, you may request that your checks be numbered beginning at a number other than 101. Frequently, this request will be denied on new accounts. However, if you are successful, the use of higher-numbered checks may keep the recipients of your checks from being tipped off that you are a new business.

OTHER ACCOUNTS

In addition to your checking account, you may also wish to consider other types of accounts such as money market, saving, C.D.s, etc. Some have limits, and withdrawals before specified dates may impose penalties. Some are liquid and a limited number of checks can be drawn on the account without penalty as long as you maintain a minimum balance.

IN CONCLUSION

Keep in mind that all accounts need not be at the same financial institution. However, it only makes sense that the amount of business you do with any one bank will be directly proportional to the benefits you will derive from it. A good banking record, along with the establishment of rapport with management and personnel of your bank, may get you special concessions. For example, the hold on your deposits may be waived if the management so desires. If you already have a bank with which you have been satisfied, you may wish to deal with them as you already have the advantage of being known by them as a valued customer. Selection of the right bank will be a definite asset to your business.

CHOOSING A BANK

	FINANCIAL INSTITUTIONS CONSIDERED		
1. DOES BANK PAY INTEREST ON CHECKING ACCT BAL?			
2. WHAT IS THE CURRENT INTEREST RATE?			
3. DOES BANK HAVE A SERVICE CHARGE?			
4. WHAT IS THE CHARGE FOR BOUNCED CHECKS?			
5. DOES BANK HAVE A HOLDING PERIOD ON DEPOSITS?			
6. DOES BANK ISSUE A CHECK GUARANTEE CARD?			
7. DOES BANK HAVE A MAJOR CREDIT CARD SERVICE?			
8. DOES BANK HAVE AN AUTO TELLER?			
9. WHAT ARE THE BANK'S HOURS OF OPERATION?			
10. DOES BANK HAVE OTHER BRANCHES?			
11. WHAT OTHER SERVICES DOES BANK OFFER?			
12. IS THE BANK IN A GOOD LOCATION?			
13. DOES THE BANK HAVE A NOTARY SERVICE?			
14. WHAT IS YOUR OVERALL FEELING ABOUT THIS BANK?			

11.

FINANCING YOUR BUSINESS

11. FINANCING YOUR BUSINESS

Financial planning is critical to the success of your business. You must know in advance how much everything connected with your business will cost and where you will get the money needed to accomplish your goals.

The first order of priority is to determine the cash available to you. The money to finance your business can come from your personal savings. Be sure that you can spare this cash. It may be awhile before a profit can be noticed. Generally, profits are put back into the business to make it grow and to increase its stability. It usually isn't advisable to quit your regular job and dive whole-heartedly into your new venture until you have thoroughly researched and test-marketed the new business.

You may be able to take a part-time job and put the added income aside for the costs of starting your business. If the job is in an area related in some way to your business, all the better!

Money can be borrowed from friends and relatives. If you choose this option, be advised that you will be closely watched, your every business decision judged, and you will have the increased stress of having to answer for all of your actions! Friends and relatives usually do not view themselves as disinterested investors; they become integral members of the management of the business which can complicate your legal structure. If you accept a loan from a friend or relative, by all means, make out a contract specifying the method of repayment, the terms of interest, and the lender's sphere of interest in the business. Then have it notarized.

Loans can be obtained through banks or the Small Business Administration. Remember that if you are a sole proprietor or in a partnership, your ability to repay will be based on your personal financial statement. Contact banks in your area to determine interest rates and loan policies.

If you have chosen to form a corporation, money can be raised through the sale of stock. **Venture capital** is another means of raising money. While banks look to the immediate future of the business in terms of repayment, venture capitalists look for long term gains. Venture capital is a risky business because of the difficulty in judging new businesses. Most venture capitalists set rigorous procedures for evaluating new businesses. When you have determined the amount of cash available to you, it is time to look at the costs involved in your business.

START-UP COSTS

Start-up costs can vary, but usually include the business license, the DBA filing fee, printing costs for business cards, brochures, and bank charges. You can get a good estimate on these costs by calling the appropriate agencies or businesses. At this time you can also get the estimates for your office supplies. Most of this can be done over the phone and can save you time. Keep a file for evaluation and follow up on those companies who offer the best prices.

OPERATING EXPENSES

Operating expenses cover a wide range and care should be taken to attach a realistic value to each of item. Following are some of the operating expenses you may need to consider.

> 1. **Rent or mortgage payments** - If you are a home-based business, figure the square footage of the area used exclusively for your business and calculate the percentage in relation to the total square footage of your home. For example, if your work room or office is 20 feet by 10 feet, it contains 200 square feet. If the total square footage of your home is 2000 square feet, the workroom/office is 10% of your home and you may calculate 10% of your mortgage interest or rent payment as a business expense.
>
> 2. **Taxes** - Taxes on a business location outside the home must be considered at full value. As in the previous example, ten percent of your property taxes would be deductible for a home office.
>
> 3. **Salaries** - If you have employees, consider not only their salaries, but also the employer's share of social security, unemployment insurance, workman's compensation, and fringe benefits such as paid holidays and disability insurance. Contract laborers or independent contractors are paid for piecework and receive no fringe benefits. You do not contribute to their social security. To be considered a valid contract laborer, strict guidelines must be followed as set forth by the I.R.S. and the Department of Labor. Contact the appropriate agency for their guidelines.

4. **Advertising** - There are many forms of advertising. Please refer to the advertising section of this book, work up a tentative plan, and figure your costs.

5. **Utilities** - Heat, electricity, and water can be evaluated by the percent amount for home-based businesses. If you do not have a separate business phone in the home, you will be expected to keep a log of calls and calculate expenses. For a business outside the home, all utilities are fully deducted.

6. **Maintenance** - Repairs and cleaning of your store or office and equipment are also expenses to be considered.

7. **Depreciation of Equipment** - Large cost items may be depreciated over time, while small cost items may be costed out in the year of purchase. Refer to the I.R.S. codes covering the current handling of depreciation.

8. **Bad accounts and collection expenses** - The owner either has to absorb the cost of a bad check or unpaid account, or pay a lawyer or collection agency to obtain payment.

9. **Insurance** - Home-based businesses should again use the percentage amount of the home-owner's policy. Insurance specific to the business is considered for full premium.

10. **Interest** on money borrowed.

11. **Stationery and supplies** - This includes all business forms, price stickers, correspondence supplies, etc.

12. **Shipping supplies** - This area includes shipping cartons, packing materials, tape and labels. These costs can be recovered by a shipping and handling fee charged to the customer.

13. **Losses due to theft, spoilage, or breakage** - You will have to estimate these amounts for the first year. Keep a record of losses for your second year budget.

14. **Travel expenses** - Retailers' buying trips and servicemen's trips to jobs are among the expenses considered. Keep a log of all business-related travel.

15. **Bank Charges** include monthly service fees and check printing costs.

COST OF GOODS SOLD

Cost of goods sold is the cost incurred to produce or acquire the products that are to be sold. You should get estimates and price lists from suppliers. Keep a card file on all of them. The ones you choose to deal with may suddenly stop carrying an item essential to your business. If you have kept an updated card file on suppliers, you'll be able to restock and continue business. Include all the raw materials that may go into the making of your product. If you don't figure all of your costs, you may be giving things away. Pass costs on to the customer.

COST OF SERVICES PROVIDED

Cost of services provided covers all costs incurred in order to provide your service. Include parts and consumable supplies such as cleaning fluids, paints, etc.

EQUIPMENT

Equipment used in your business such as a typewriter, tools, etc.

WAGE OR DRAW

This is your means of getting money out of your business. You may choose to pay yourself an hourly wage or a salary. This is sometimes difficult in a small business which is just starting out and may have a cash flow problem. You may choose to take a draw which means taking a portion of the profit from the company for your own use when the company budget is healthy.

SETTING A PRICE

Setting a price for your product or service will be one of your biggest considerations. You want to be competitive and also make a profit. There is little in print to help you price new products. Generally, product makers have to rely on their own intuition and marketing knowledge to arrive at a good price. Two of the easiest formulas follow and cover the means of arriving at an hourly rate to charge in a service industry and a method for determining the wholesale price of a product.

In her book, **HOMEMADE MONEY**, Barbara Brabec presents one of the best formulas for determining an hourly rate. It was originally formulated by Libby Platus and published in **THE CRAFTS REPORT**. The **hourly rate formula** can be used to determine how much to charge per hour if you are providing a service. You will need to determined your desired annual net income. How much profit would you like to have at the end of the year? Also figure out how many hours you want to work per year on the service you will provide. Be sure to include the hours spent on office work, errand running, and other miscellaneous business-related work. Now compute a figure for your annual expenses based on a total from your estimates on the amount of cash to be paid out.

The formula is the **desired annual net income** divided by the **number of hours worked per year**. This amount is added to the **annual expenses** divided by the **number of hours worked per year**. This formula will give you the hourly rate you must charge in order to realize your desired net income. **Don't panic** — it's not as hard as it seems! When the problem is set up, it looks as follows:

> **Desired annual net income $10,000**
> **Number of hours worked per year = 1,000**
> **(20 hours per week X 50 weeks)**
> **Annual expenses = $8,000**

$$\frac{\text{Desired annual net income } \$10{,}000}{1{,}000 \text{ Numbers of hours worked per year}} + \frac{\text{Annual Expenses } \$8{,}000}{1{,}000 \text{ Number of hours worked per year}}$$

$10.00 + $8.00 = $18.00 per hour

In order to net $10,000 per year, you will have to work 1,000 hours per year and charge $18.00 per hour. This formula allows for flexibility. Do you want to make more profit? Then you can work more hours per year. If you do this, be sure to increase your annual expenses accordingly. If you work more hours, you will be increasing the use of utilities, consumable supplies, etc. A decrease in your annual expenses will decrease the rate per hour. This is to your advantage. You can still charge $18.00 per hour. The difference is a bonus! Perhaps $18.00 is too much to charge based on your competition. Lower your annual net income, lower your annual expenses, or work more hours. Examples of the flexibility of this formula can be found at the end of this section.

The **formula for manufacturers** will help you determine a wholesale value for your product. You will need to compute the cost of your labor. Figure the amount of time needed to make one item and the amount of hourly wage to be paid for its production. Be realistic! What would you pay a contract laborer or an employee? Now determine the cost of materials for making one unit. Figure how many units one person could produce per year. Estimate your annual overhead and your desired annual profit.

The formula is the **cost of labor** plus the **cost of materials for one unit** times the **number of units to be produced in one year**. Add this amount to the **annual overhead** plus the **desired annual profit**. Now divide that quantity by the **number of units to produced in one year**. This will give you the wholesale price you must charge to reach your desired annual income. When the formula is set up, it will be as follows:

>Cost of labor per item = $2.50
>(Compute the amount of time needed to make one item. In this example, one half hour. Figure the hourly wage. In this case, $5.00. The cost labor per item would be $2.50.)
>
>Cost of materials for one unit = $2.00
>Number of units produced per year = 2,000
>Estimated annual overhead = $4,000
>Desired annual profit = $10,000

$$\frac{\text{(No. of units produced per year) } 2{,}000 \times [\text{Cost of labor } \$2.50 + \text{Materials for 1 unit } \$2.00] + \text{Annual overhead } \$4{,}000 + \text{Desired annual profit } \$10{,}000}{\text{No. of units produced per year } 2{,}000}$$

$$\frac{[2{,}000 \times \$4.50] + 4{,}000 + \$10{,}000}{2{,}000} \quad \frac{23{,}000}{2{,}000} = \$11.50 \text{ (Wholesale price)}$$

Most stores will keystone or double the wholesale price to arrive at a retail price. Since your wholesale price is $11.50, you can assume a retail price of $23.00. Perhaps this is too high for the consumer. You may want to consider adjusting some of the figures you are using. Examples of the flexibility of this formula are shown at the end of this section.

These formulas and examples are offered as guides in helping you in determining your wholesale product price and hourly service rate. They are only as accurate as the figures being used. Your marketing plan will help you to be realistic about projecting the number of units which can be sold in a year as well as the price which will be realistic in the marketplace.

When you have determined the amount of cash available, have computed all of your costs, and have figured your hourly rate or price of product, you must view your business venture objectively. Is what you are planning to do cost-effective? If not, look for ways to lower costs or increase prices. You certainly don't want a negative cash flow and now is a good time to make the adjustments necessary to ensure a profit and not a loss.

SOURCES OF CASH WORKSHEET

(CASH FLOWING INTO YOUR BUSINESS)

1. **CASH ON HAND** $ _____

2. **SALES·REVENUES**
   Sales   _____
   Service Income   _____
   Deposits on Sales or Services   _____
   Collections on Accounts Receivable   _____

3. **MISCELLANEOUS INCOME**
   Interest Income   _____

4. **SALE OF LONG-TERM ASSETS**   _____

5. **LIABILITIES**
   Loans (Banks, Finance Cos., S.B.A., etc.)   _____

6. **EQUITY**
   Owner Investments (Sole Prop. or Partnership)   _____
   Contributed Capital (Corporation)   _____
   Sale of Stock (Corporation)   _____
   Venture Capital   _____

   TOTAL CASH AVAILABLE . . . . $ _____

CASH TO BE PAID OUT WORKSHEET
(CASH FLOWING OUT OF YOUR BUSINESS)

START-UP COSTS:
    Business License (annual expense) $_____
    DBA Filing Fee (one-time cost)   _____
    Other start-up costs:
    _____   _____
    _____   _____
    _____   _____

INVENTORY PURCHASES   _____
    Cash out for items for resale or services

SELLING EXPENSE (DIRECT EXPENSE)
    Advertising   _____
    Freight   _____
    Packaging Costs   _____
    Parts & Supplies   _____
    Sales Salaries   _____
    Misc. Direct Exp.   _____
  TOTAL DIRECT EXPENSE   _____

OPERATING EXPENSE (INDIRECT EXPENSE)
    Depreciation Expense   _____
    Insurance   _____
    Licenses & Permits   _____
    Office Salaries   _____
    Rent Expense   _____
    Utilities   _____
    Miscell. Indirect Exp.   _____
  TOTAL INDIRECT EXPENSE   _____

ASSETS (LONG-TERM PURCHASES)   _____
    Cash to be paid in current period

LIABILITIES   _____
    Cash outlay for retiring debts, loans,
    and/or accounts payable

OWNER EQUITY   _____
    Cash to be withdrawn by owner

        TOTAL CASH TO BE PAID OUT . . . . . $_____

Note: Be sure to use the same time period throughout your worksheets---monthly, quarterly annually.

Financing Your Business

SAMPLE FINANCIAL STATEMENT
(Personal)

PERSONAL FINANCIAL STATEMENT

(DO NOT USE FOR BUSINESS)

As of _____ _____ 19 _____

Received at _____ Branch

Name _____ Employed by _____ Years _____

Address _____ Position _____ Age ____ Name of Spouse _____

If Employed Less Than 1 Year, Previous Employer _____

The undersigned, for the purpose of procuring and establishing credit from time to time with you and to induce you to permit the undersigned to become indebted to you on notes, endorsements, guarantees, overdrafts or otherwise, furnishes the following (or in lieu thereof the attached) which is the most recent statement prepared by or for the undersigned as being a full, true and correct statement of the financial condition of the undersigned on the date indicated, and agrees to notify you immediately of the extent and character of any material change in said financial condition, and also agrees that if the undersigned, or any endorser or guarantor of any of the obligations of the undersigned, at any time fails in business or becomes insolvent, or commits an act of bankruptcy, or dies, or if a writ of attachment, garnishment, execution or other legal process be issued against property of the undersigned or if any assessment for taxes against the undersigned, other than taxes on real property, is made by the federal or state government or any department thereof, or if any of the representations made below prove to be untrue, or if the undersigned fails to notify you of any material change as above agreed, or if such change occurs, or if the business, or any interest therein, of the undersigned is sold, then and in such case, all of the obligations of the undersigned to you or held by you shall immediately be due and payable, without demand or notice. This statement shall be construed by you to be a continuing statement of the condition of the undersigned, and a new and original statement of all assets and liabilities upon each and every transaction in and by which the undersigned hereafter becomes indebted to you, until the undersigned advises in writing to the contrary.

ASSETS	DOLLARS	cents	LIABILITIES	DOLLARS	cents
Cash in B of _____ (Branch)			Notes payable B of _____ (Branch)		
Cash in _____ (Other - give name)			Notes payable _____ (Other)		
Accounts Receivable-Good _____			Accounts payable _____		
Stocks and Bonds (Schedule B) _____			Taxes payable _____		
Notes Receivable-Good _____			Contracts payable _____ (To whom)		
Cash Surrender Value Life Insurance _____			Contracts payable _____ (To whom)		
Autos _____ (Year-Make) _____ (Year-Make)			Real Estate indebtedness (Schedule A) _____		
Real Estate (Schedule A) _____			Other Liabilities (describe)		
Other Assets (describe)			1. _____		
1. _____			2. _____		
2. _____			3. _____		
3. _____			4. _____		
4. _____			TOTAL LIABILITIES		
5. _____			NET WORTH		
TOTAL ASSETS			**TOTAL**		

ANNUAL INCOME and **ANNUAL EXPENDITURES** (Excluding Ordinary living expenses)

ANNUAL INCOME	DOLLARS	cents	ANNUAL EXPENDITURES	DOLLARS	cents
Salary _____			Real Estate payment(s) _____		
Salary (wife or husband) _____			Rent _____		
Securities Income _____			Income Taxes _____		
Rentals _____			Insurance Premiums _____		
Other (describe)			Property Taxes _____		
1. _____			Other (describe-include instalment payments other than real estate)		
2. _____			1. _____		
3. _____			2. _____		
4. _____			3. _____		
5. _____					
TOTAL INCOME			**TOTAL EXPENDITURES**		
LESS-TOTAL EXPENDITURES					
NET CASH INCOME (exclusive of ordinary living expenses) _____					

SAMPLE

SAMPLE FINANCIAL STATEMENT - page 2
(Personal)

What assets in this statement are in joint tenancy? _____ Name of other Party _____

Have you filed homestead? _____

Are you a guarantor on anyone's debt? _____ If so, give details _____

Are any encumbered assets or debts secured except as indicated? _____ If so, please itemize by debt and security _____

Do you have any other business connections? _____ If so, give details _____

Are there any suits or judgments against you? _____ Any pending? _____

Have you gone through bankruptcy or compromised a debt? _____

Have you made a will? _____ Number of dependents _____

SCHEDULE A—REAL ESTATE

Location and type of Improvement	Title in Name of	Estimated Value	Amount Owing	To Whom Payable

SCHEDULE B—STOCKS AND BONDS

Number of Shares Amount of Bonds	Description	Current Market on Listed	Estimated Value on Unlisted
		$	$

If additional space is needed for Schedule A and/or Schedule B, list on separate sheet and attach.

INSURANCE

Life Insurance $ _____ Name of Company _____ Beneficiary _____

Automobile Insurance:
Public Liability — yes ☐   no ☐   Property Damage — yes ☐   no ☐
Comprehensive personal Liability — yes ☐   no ☐

STATEMENT OF BANK OFFICER:

Insofar as our records reveal, this Financial Statement is accurate and true. The foregoing statement is (a copy of) the original signed by the maker, in the credit files of this bank.

_____ Assistant Cashier Manager

The undersigned certifies that the above statement (or in lieu thereof, the attached statement, as the case may be) and supporting schedules, both printed and written, give a full, true, and correct statement of the financial condition of the undersigned as of the date indicated.

Date signed _____   Signature _____

Financing Your Business

HOURLY RATE FORMULA

$$\frac{\text{Desired Annual Net Income} + \text{Annual Expenses}}{\text{Number of Working Hours Per Year}}$$

BASE FIGURES:

Desired annual net income = $10,000
No. Working hours per year = 1,000   = $18.00 per hour
Annual overhead = $8,000

TO LOWER REQUIRED HOURLY RATE:

1. Decrease Desired Annual Net Income
2. Decrease Annual Expenses
3. Increase Number of Working Hours Per Year

THE HOURLY RATE YOU CAN CHARGE IS DETERMINED BY:

1. What the market will bear for your particular industry
2. Your quality of service to your customer.
3. The uniqueness of your service.

If the required hourly rate is too high, you will have to work with the formula until you bring it down to a figure that will keep you in the marketplace.

Note: Do not fail to consider all of the expenses incurred in operating your business. (Direct Expenses, Indirect Expenses, Interest Expenses, and Income and Self-Employment Taxes)

FORMULA FOR MANUFACTURERS

$$\frac{\text{No. of units produced per year} \times [\text{Cost of labor} + \text{Materials for 1 unit}] + \text{Estimated Annual Overhead} + \text{Desired Annual Profit}}{\text{Number of Units per Year}}$$

BASE FIGURES:
Cost of labor = $1.50 per unit
Cost of materials = $2.00 per unit
No. units per year = 20,000
Estimated annual overhead = $75,000
   (a. $20,000 Direct Expenses, b. $28,000 Indirect Expenses,
   c. $5,000 Interest Expense, d. $22,000 Taxes)
Desired Annual Profit = $50,000

USING THE ABOVE FORMULA:

A. $\dfrac{20{,}000 \times (\$1.50 + \$2.00) + \$75{,}000 + \$50{,}000}{20{,}000} =$ Wholesale Price

B. $\dfrac{\$50{,}000 + \$75{,}000 + \$50{,}000}{20{,}000} = \$8.75$ Wholesale Price

TO LOWER THE WHOLESALE PRICE:

1. Increase Number of Units Produced Per Year.
2. Decrease cost of labor per unit.
3. Decrease cost of materials per unit.
4. Lower Annual Overhead.
5. Decrease desired annual profit.

THE SELLING PRICE OF YOUR PRODUCT IS DETERMINED BY WHAT THE MARKET WILL BEAR! You cannot exceed the selling price or you will price yourself out of the market. To determine that price, you will have to do market research, untilzing such tools as questionnaires, demographics, competition analysis, and test marketing. You can then work within the framework of the formula, increasing or decreasing its components to arrive at the desired selling price. Ultimate success will be dependent on your ability to realize these projections.

Financing Your Business

12.

KEEPING RECORDS

12. KEEPING RECORDS

The keeping of accurate records is imperative if your business is to succeed. Your records have two main functions. The first is to provide you with information that will help you to see the trends that are taking place within your operation. If you have a simple but complete set of records, it will be possible for you to tell at a glance what is happening with your business — which areas are productive and cost-effective and which will require change. For this reason, a new business owner should have a hands-on system rather than delegating this job to an outsider. Keeping your own books and records will make you doubly aware of what is going on in your business. The second function of recordkeeping is to provide you with income tax information. Failure to be able to retrieve and verify that information can cause you and your accountant a multitude of problems and may result in audits, penalties and even the termination of your business.

TYPES OF RECORDKEEPING

The system you use must be tailored to your individual needs. Because no two businesses will have exactly the same concerns, it is best that you do not buy a ready-made set of books. Consider the factors that you will want to have on hand and set up your records accordingly. In all systems, you will have to keep track of income and expenses. Your needs will include such items as general ledger, petty cash system, inventory record, receipt file, checkbook and customer file, when appropriate. The text in this chapter is followed by samples of most of these types of records, as well as sample income tax schedules, a list of common tax deductions, a record retention schedule, a general recordkeeping schedule, and miscellaneous samples which may prove helpful to you when you set up your own recordkeeping. Whatever your system, it is important to keep in mind that simplicity is the key to small business accounting. Fewer records are easier to read and they will require less bookkeeping time.

INCOME

Income is all the monies received by your business in any given period of time. It is made up of retail sales, wholesale sales, sale of services and any miscellaneous income. A simple formula for recordkeeping is that **income equals deposits.** Do not use monies received to purchase goods and plan to deposit the rest. It is interesting to note that the IRS does not require you to keep copies of your receipt books if you follow this formula. It is also interesting to note that the 1987 Tax Reform supports the importance of using the above-mentioned income equals deposits equation.

EXPENSES

Expenses fall into two general categories — those paid by check and those paid with cash. The latter should be small incidental purchases and are known as Petty Cash. These transactions, as well as those paid by check, require careful recording. The keeping of a Petty Cash Record will be discussed in following text.

TAX REGULATIONS

Tax regulations are the nemesis of every red-blooded American. You should make every attempt to study all the regulations pertaining to your business. Review the appropriate tax forms for the current year and familiarize yourself with IRS deductions. Failure to utilize all of your deductions can make the difference between profit and loss for the fiscal year. A partial list of common tax deductions for small business can be found in the samples at the end of the chapter. Self-employed persons should note that they must file quarterly estimated returns. Net income for each quarter is estimated and payments made on the appropriate dates to the IRS and to the state in which you do business, unless that state has no income tax. Samples of the Estimated Tax Vouchers and a Computation Schedule are included herein along with other sample forms to be filed with your yearly tax returns. (Schedule C for a sole proprietorship, Schedule 1065 for a partnership, etc.) Please look at the end of this chapter.

SETTING UP YOUR RECORDS

Setting up your records must take place immediately upon the onset of your business dealings. Do not think you will be able to go about your business and then go back and catch up on the bookkeeping. Record and file any information that might possibly be pertinent. If you find out later that changes need to be made, you can revamp your system as necessary. Most records have a suggested retention period. For your convenience we have included a Records Retention Schedule. To help you with the setting up of your recordkeeping, the following paragraphs will be devoted to those books and records which we feel should be a part of most small and home-based businesses.

1. GENERAL JOURNAL A General Journal is kept to record transactions made by your business. These transactions are recorded in the form of debits and credits. **Debits** are all monies paid out. **Credits** are all monies received. The General Ledger should have enough columns to cover major categories of expenses and income. A twelve-column ledger will suffice for most small businesses. Note that these categories may change with your needs and as you refine your recordkeeping system. In addition to major expense columns, you must have a Petty Cash column and a Miscellaneous column. Both may be handled under the Miscellaneous column as long as proper notation is made for later division of expenses for tax purposes. We would suggest that you use a system in your General Journal in which each entry is made twice — once under the Debit or Credit column and once under the appropriate corresponding income or expense column. (Ex.: Enter the purchase of postage stamps under Debit and also under Office Supplies.) This provides a check for accuracy when balancing at the end of each ledger page and keeps errors from being perpetuated and difficult to find at a later time. When making corrections in the Journal cross out and initial changes. Be careful and do your work legibly so it can be read and interpreted with ease. At the end of the month, compute the totals of all columns and transfer the Debit and Credit totals to the Profit and Loss Sheet. This sheet will provide a picture of what has happened during each month. Comparison of two or more years' Profit and Loss Sheets can quickly show you the general trend in business at certain times of the year. Note: Samples of a General Journal page and a Profit and Loss Sheet are found following the text.

2. PETTY CASH RECORD - A petty cash fund should be used to pay small amounts for purchases when it is not practical to pay by check. A check is drawn and debited to Petty Cash in the General Journal (See General Journal sample). That amount is credited in the Petty Cash Record as a deposit. When cash purchases are made, they are debited to petty cash by recording them as expenses. When the fund gets low, another check is drawn to rebuild the fund. It is imperative that all receipts are filed and easily retrievable. It should be noted that these expenses are later divided into classifications for tax purposes. Because a large Miscellaneous deduction may be suspect and cause your return to be selected for audit by the IRS, we suggest that you divide your Petty Cash Record into the following categories so that individual purchases may be credited to their appropriate expense accounts:

      a. Date of transaction
      b. Purchased from
      c. Expense account to be debited

d. Deposit
e. Amount of Expense
f. Balance of the Fund

A sample page of this type is included. If you have purchased any items that need entering in other records (Ex.: Inventory, Tools, etc.), do so when you debit petty cash. This will keep these records current and eliminate omitting them by mistake.

Mention should be made at this time that petty cash purchases are easy to forget. They can account for a significant portion of your business expenses. Careful attention to this matter will make a significant difference in your deductible expenses at the end of the business year. By all means, be meticulous about this fund.

3. **INVENTORY RECORD** - The keeping of an Inventory Record is definitely required. Small items can be expenses at the end of the year, but larger items, such as office equipment, tools, goods purchased for resale and other pertinent purchases should be inventoried in separate records. A small business may find that a simple lined book will have enough pages to be divided into sections with colored tabs and used for recording inventories, petty cash, trips, etc., keeping your number of books at a minimum. At the end of the year, some inventoried items are expensed out. Others are depreciated. Please note that those used as **depreciable items may not also be used as direct expenses.** Most depreciable purchases are those in excess of $100.00. Those items purchased for resale must be recorded in a separate inventory. This record is used to determine Beginning and Ending Inventories for the tax year. Examination of Schedule C (included) will show that these figures are used by the IRS to determine your net profit in sales. Your inventory records will also show what goods you have on hand at any given time. These records should be stored in a safe place as they may be used by an insurance company in case of loss. Your Inventory Record should have the following columns:

a. Purchase Date
b. Item Purchased
c. Purchase Price
d. Date Sold
e. Sale Price
f. Sales Tax

The last three items are for goods purchased for resale. A sample Inventory Record is included.

4. **FILES** - As was mentioned in an earlier paragraph, your records must be filed and retained until they are no longer useful. Your files should be organized with easy retrieval as a prerequisite. Most small businesses need no more than a two-drawer file cabinet, an accordion receipt file and some type of portable file to comprise their system The records in the file cabinet can be divided into categories with file folders. These files may have names such as Invoices Payable, Invoices Receivable, Pending, Office Equipment, etc. The accordion file can be used for all receipts and should preferably have pockets divided into alphabetical letters A-Z. Your portable file will be used when you have to transport certain records from one place to another. With the use of file folders, it is a simple matter to pick out the files you need and transfer them into your portable file.

5. **CHECKBOOK** - Having a business checking account keeps your personal and business finances separate. This is a must for the success of any business. The checkbook you choose should be of a style and size to meet your specific needs. Your bank can help you with your selection. Some businesses use the larger business-type book. Others prefer to use the small pocket-type that can be more easily carried with you. Personally, I like the book type as it contains more room for information. Whatever type you choose, write enough information in your register so that you can quickly recall the important details of your transaction should the need arise.

6. **CUSTOMER RECORDS** - In order to protect the customer and the business, it may be necessary to keep some sort of customer records. This is especially true in a service-oriented business. For example, if you are an appliance repair business, it would be advantageous to keep a record of the work done, the date it was done and the amount charged for the repair. If the customer has a problem at a later time, it is easy to see if it is related to the work done and whether or not the present problem should be covered under your guarantee. This protects the customer if he has lost his receipt — and you if the customer's recall is less than accurate. If your business is not set-up with a computer, box files that hold 3x5 index cards can serve as efficient customer files.

END OF YEAR

At the end of the tax year you will need to bring all of your recordkeeping together in order to review your business year and retrieve information for income tax purposes. As we stated before, a review of the appropriate tax forms for your type of business will provide you with the clues as to what information you will need. At this time, it is probably a good idea to work with an accountant to determine all information needed to help you maximize your tax benefits. If you are unable to do all the preliminary tax work, it may cost you very little to have the final tax computations done and your tax returns prepared by a professional whose business it is to know all the current tax laws and how to apply them. With all the changes that are continually being made in our tax structure, it is almost impossible for the ordinary individual to understand all of the laws and how to apply them to his or her income tax returns. After you have completed your returns, that year's records should be stored together. If you are ever called to audit, it will be easy to find the information pertaining to the tax return in question.

BALANCE SHEET

Mention should be made at this point that many businesses use the Balance Sheet as one of their principal financial statements prepared from the ledgers and records of their businesses. The Balance Sheet is usually prepared at the close of the business year. It lists Assets, Liabilities, and Capital. At the end of each fiscal year the accounts are balanced and closed. Income and Expense Account balances are transferred to the Summary of Revenue and Expenses (included) and are used in the Income Statement. The remaining Asset, Liability, and Capital information derived from your records provides the figures for the Balance Sheet. The following are samples of accounts used to prepare a Balance Sheet:

ASSETS

Cash in Bank, Petty Cash, Accounts Receivable, Inventory, Supplies on Hand, Deposits, Land, Buildings, Accounts Depreciable (buildings, equipment, furniture, automotive; all credits), Furniture, Fixtures

LIABILITIES

Accounts Payable, Sales Tax Payable, FICA Taxes Payable, Federal and State Withholding Taxes, Miscellaneous Accruals

CAPITAL ACCOUNTS

For Corporation - Common and Preferred Capital Stock
Proprietorships - Proprietorship Account and Proprietor Withdrawals
Retained Earnings

Note: 2 samples of a Balance Sheet and Income Statement are included in the material at the end of this chapter. The balance Sheet will be a necessity in the event that you have the need to present an overall picture of the **current** financial status of your business. The Income Statement will show a moving picture of your business for the past financial period.

RECORDKEEPING SCHEDULE

In order that you may better utilize the information that we have given to you in the previous pages of this chapter, we have prepared and included a General Recordkeeping Schedule. If you have set up the books, records and files that have been discussed in this section, you will be able to follow the Recordkeeping Schedule, using it as a guide throughout the year. You should have a simple, accurate system that will enable you to retrieve information quickly. It will also provide you with an accurate picture of what is happening with your business. Keep in mind that you may need some types of records that are not discussed in this text. Each business has its individual needs and it would be presumptuous to think that we could discuss them all here. You must decide what it is that you need and set up your recordkeeping accordingly.

SUMMARY

If we have accomplished nothing more in this section than to impress upon you the value of good recordkeeping, we will consider ourselves successful. Remember that simple and accurate recordkeeping is your most valuable asset. In succeeding years, examination of those records and comparison of those records from preceding years will reveal your strengths and weaknesses. It will be easy to see the trends in all phases of your business and to utilize that information in planning the future. Your business success will be measured in two ways, in personal satisfaction and financial gain. The measure of personal satisfaction is in your heart. The measure of your financial gain is readily seen in the **RECORDS YOU SO CAREFULLY KEPT!!!**

COMMON DEDUCTIBLE EXPENSES

(For Small and Home-Based Businesses)

Note: Please read the text that follows this form for more information on deductions. There may be other expenses which apply to your business. Those listed below are the most common deductions.

DEDUCTIONS TO BE EXPENSED

ADVERTISING – yellow pages, newspaper, radio, mail.
BAD DEBTS – from sales or services
BANK SERVICE CHARGES – Checks, etc.
BOOKS AND PERIODICALS – business-rel.
CAR & TRUCK EXPENSES – gas, repair, ins., license fee, maintenance.
COMMISSIONS – to sales reps.
CONTRACT SERVICES – independent.
CONVENTION EXPENSES
DISPLAY & EXHIBITOR'S EXPENSES
DONATIONS
DUES – professional
EDUCATIONAL FEES & MATERIALS
ELECTRIC BILLS
ENTERTAINMENT OF CLIENTS
FREIGHT – UPS, Postal, etc.
GAS BILLS
IMPROVEMENTS – under $100.00
INSURANCE – business-related.
INTEREST PAID OUT
LAUNDRY & CLEANING – uniforms, et.
LEGAL & PROFESSIONAL FEES
LICENSE FEE – business license
MAINTENANCE – materials & labor
OFFICE EQUIPMENT – under $100.00.
OFFICE FURNITURE – under $100.00.
OFFICE SUPPLIES
PARKING FEES
PENSION & PROFIT-SHARING PLANS
POSTAGE
PRINTING EXPENSES
PROFESSIONAL SERVICES
PROMOTIONAL MATERIALS

PROPERTY TAX
PUBLICATIONS
REPAIRS
REFUNDS, RETURNS & ALLOWANCES
SALES TAX – sales tax collected is Income and the reimbursement to SBE is deducted as expense.
SALES TAX PAID — on purchases.
SUBSCRIPTIONS
TELEPHONE
TOOLS – used in trade and with purchase price under $100.00.
UNIFORMS PURCHASED
UTILITIES see gas, electric & telephone
WAGES PAID OUT

TO BE DEPRECIATED

BUSINESS PROPERTY
OFFICE FURNITURE – over $100
OFFICE EQUIPMENT – over $100
VEHICLES – used solely for business purposes.
TOOLS – over $100
TANGIBLE PURCHASES – used for business and costing over $100 (not purchases for resale).

COMMON DEDUCTIBLE EXPENSES
(For Small & Home-Based Businesses)

The list of common tax-deductible expenses was prepared to help you identify many of those items which are **normally** deductible for income tax purposes. The new business owner should become familiar with those appropriate to the business. **DO NOT** wait until tax preparation time to look at this list. Knowing ahead of time which expenses are deductible will help you to better utilize them to your advantage while keeping proper records for income tax verification. **DO** keep in mind that this is only a partial list. There may very well be additional deductible expenses relating to your business. Call or visit the IRS. They have free publications and there are experts available to answer your questions. Another source of information is your accountant. Be sure to have documentation for all expenses so you can verify them if you are audited.

DEDUCTIBLE BUSINESS EXPENSES fall into two major categories: 1. Those which are deductible in their entirety in the year in which they are incurred, and 2. Those items considered depreciable, costing in excess of $100.00 and used in the operation of your business.

> **1. Fully-deductible expenses** - All expenses incurred in the operation of your business are deductible and reduce your net income by their amount unless they are major expenses that fall in the depreciable category. These expenses will have to be itemized for tax purposes, and receipts should be easily retrievable for verification purposes.
>
> **2. Depreciable expenses** - A rule of thumb is that those items costing in excess of $100.00 and used in connection with your business will be expensed through depreciation. Those assets generally include such things as office equipment, buildings, vehicles, etc. The Tax Reform 1987 contains strict rulings on depreciation. Information is available through the IRS. Depreciation is taken at a fixed rate and that portion allowed for the current year is deducted as an expense. It should be noted again that you **MAY NOT** use that item as both a fully-deductible expense and a depreciation expense. For example, a desk purchased for $500.00 in 1986 will have to be depreciated according to schedule at $100.00 per year for 5 years. If your total office equipment expense was $972.00, you must subtract the $500.00 leaving you with $472.00 fully-deductible expense for the year. The $100.00 depreciation for the desk is accounted for under depreciation expense. The additional $400.00 cost of the desk will be expensed equally to the next four years as depreciation.

HOME-BASED BUSINESSES - In order for your home to qualify as a business expense, that part of your home used in business pursuits must be used exclusively and on a regular basis in your work. For further information, you may dial the IRS Tele-Tax Information in your area or send for the free IRS Publication #587, "Business Use of Your Home".

Keeping Records

ESTIMATED TAX WORKSHEET SAMPLE

1988 Estimated Tax Worksheet (Keep for Your Records—Do Not Send to Internal Revenue Service)

1	Enter amount of Adjusted Gross Income you expect in 1988.	1
2	If you plan to itemize deductions, enter the estimated total of your deductions. If you do not plan to itemize deductions, see **Standard Deduction** on page 3. Enter the amount here	2
3	Subtract line 2 from line 1. Enter the difference here	3
4	Exemptions (multiply $1,950 times number of personal exemptions). If you are eligible to be claimed as a dependent on another person's return, see **Personal Exemption** on page 3	4
5	Subtract line 4 from line 3.	5
6	Tax. (Figure your tax on line 5 by using Tax Rate Schedule X, Y, or Z in these instructions. DO NOT use the Tax Table or Tax Rate Schedule X, Y, or Z in the 1987 Form 1040 instructions.)	6
7	Enter any additional taxes (see line 7 instructions)	7
8	Add lines 6 and 7.	8
9	Credits (see line 9 instructions)	9
10	Subtract line 9 from line 8.	10
11	Self-employment tax. Estimate of 1988 self-employment income $ _____ if $45,000 or more, enter $5,859; if less, multiply the amount by .1302 (see line 11 instructions)	11
12	Other taxes (see line 12 instructions)	12
13a	Total. Add lines 10 through 12	13a
b	Earned income credit and credit from **Form 4136**	13b
c	Total. Subtract line 13b from line 13a	13c
14a	Enter 90% (66 ⅔% for farmers and fishermen) of line 13c.	14a
b	Enter 100% of the tax shown on your 1987 tax return.	14b
c	Enter the smaller of lines 14a or 14b. This is your required annual payment. **Caution.** *Generally, if you do not prepay at least the amount on line 14c, you may be subject to a penalty for not paying enough estimated tax. To avoid a penalty, make sure your estimate on line 13c is as accurate as possible. If you are unsure of your estimate and line 14a is smaller than line 14b, you may want to pay up to the amount shown on line 14b. For more information, get Publication 505.*	14c
15	Income tax withheld and estimated to be withheld (including income tax withholding on pensions, annuities, certain deferred income, etc.) during 1988.	15
16	Balance (subtract line 15 from line 14c). (**Note:** If line 13c less line 15 is less than $500, you are not required to make estimated tax payments.) If you are applying an overpayment from 1987 to 1988 estimated tax, see Instruction C(2), page 1.	16
17	If the first payment you are required to make is due April 15, 1988, enter ¼ of line 16 (less any 1987 overpayment that you are applying to this installment) here and on line 1 of your payment-voucher(s). You may round off cents to the nearest whole dollar	17

Amended Estimated Tax Schedule (Use if your estimated tax changes during the year)

1	Amended estimated tax	1
2a	Amount of 1987 overpayment chosen for credit to 1988 estimated tax and applied to date	2a
b	Estimated tax payments to date	2b
c	Total of lines 2a and 2b	2c
3	Unpaid balance (subtract line 2c from line 1)	3
4	Amount to be paid (see Instructions D (1) and E)	4

Page 5

ESTIMATED TAXES - SAMPLE VOUCHERS

Form 1040-ES (OCR) Department of the Treasury Internal Revenue Service	**1988 Payment-Voucher**

Return this voucher with check or money order payable to the Internal Revenue Service.
Please do not send cash or staple your payment to this voucher.
File only if you are making a payment of estimated tax.

OMB No. 1545-0087
(Calendar year—Due April 15, 1988)

1 Amount of payment $ _____
2 Fiscal year filers
    enter year ending _____
             (month and year)

If name, address, or social security number is incorrect, please change.

For Paperwork Reduction Act Notice, see instructions on page 1.

Form 1040-ES (OCR) Department of the Treasury Internal Revenue Service	**1988 Payment-Voucher**

Return this voucher with check or money order payable to the Internal Revenue Service.
Please do not send cash or staple your payment to this voucher.
File only if you are making a payment of estimated tax.

OMB No. 1545-0087
(Calendar year—Due June 15, 1988)

1 Amount of payment $ _____
2 Fiscal year filers
    enter year ending _____
             (month and year)

If name, address, or social security no. is incorrect, and was not previously corrected, please change.

For Paperwork Reduction Act Notice, see instructions on page 1.

Form 1040-ES (OCR) Department of the Treasury Internal Revenue Service	**1988 Payment-Voucher**

Return this voucher with check or money order payable to the Internal Revenue Service.
Please do not send cash or staple your payment to this voucher.
File only if you are making a payment of estimated tax.

OMB No. 1545-0087
(Calendar year—Due Sept. 15, 1988)

1 Amount of payment $ _____
2 Fiscal year filers
    enter year ending _____
             (month and year)

If name, address, or social security no. is incorrect, and was not previously corrected, please change.

For Paperwork Reduction Act Notice, see instructions on page 1.

Form 1040-ES (OCR) Department of the Treasury Internal Revenue Service	**1988 Payment-Voucher**

Return this voucher with check or money order payable to the Internal Revenue Service.
Please do not send cash or staple your payment to this voucher.
File only if you are making a payment of estimated tax.

OMB No. 1545-0087
(Calendar year—Due Jan. 15, 1988)

1 Amount of payment $ _____
2 Fiscal year filers
    enter year ending _____
             (month and year)

If name, address, or social security no. is incorrect, and was not previously corrected, please change.

For Paperwork Reduction Act Notice, see instructions on page 1.

Keeping Records

FORM 1040 - SCHEDULE C

SAMPLE TAX RETURN FOR SOLE PROPRIETOR

SCHEDULE C (Form 1040)
Department of the Treasury
Internal Revenue Service (3)

Profit or (Loss) From Business or Profession
(Sole Proprietorship)
Partnerships, Joint Ventures, etc., Must File Form 1065.
▶ Attach to Form 1040, Form 1041, or Form 1041S. ▶ See Instructions for Schedule C (Form 1040).

OMB No. 1545-0074

1987

Attachment Sequence No. 09

Name of proprietor

Social security number (SSN)

- **A** Principal business or profession, including product or service (see Instructions)
- **B** Principal business code (from Part IV) ▶
- **C** Business name and address ▶
- **D** Employer ID number (Not SSN)
- **E** Method(s) used to value closing inventory:
  - (1) ☐ Cost
  - (2) ☐ Lower of cost or market
  - (3) ☐ Other (attach explanation)
- **F** Accounting method: (1) ☐ Cash (2) ☐ Accrual (3) ☐ Other (specify) ▶
- **G** Was there any change in determining quantities, costs, or valuations between opening and closing inventory? (If "Yes," attach explanation.)
- **H** Are you deducting expenses for an office in your home?
- **I** Did you file **Form 941** for this business for any quarter in 1987?
- **J** Did you "materially participate" in the operation of this business during 1987? (If "No," see Instructions for limitations on losses.)
- **K** Was this business in operation at the end of 1987?
- **L** How many months was this business in operation during 1987? ▶
- **M** If this schedule includes a loss, credit, deduction, income, or other tax benefit relating to a tax shelter required to be registered, check here. ▶ ☐
  If you check this box, you **MUST** attach **Form 8271**.

Part I Income

1a	Gross receipts or sales	1a
b	Less: Returns and allowances	1b
c	Subtract line 1b from line 1a and enter the balance here	1c
2	Cost of goods sold and/or operations (from Part III, line 8)	2
3	Subtract line 2 from line 1c and enter the **gross profit** here	3
4	Other income (including windfall profit tax credit or refund received in 1987)	4
5	Add lines 3 and 4. This is the **gross income** ▶	5

Part II Deductions

6	Advertising		23	Repairs	
7	Bad debts from sales or services (see Instructions.)		24	Supplies (not included in Part III)	
			25	Taxes	
8	Bank service charges		26	Travel, meals, and entertainment:	
9	Car and truck expenses		a	Travel	
10	Commissions		b	Total meals and entertainment	
11	Depletion				
12	Depreciation and section 179 deduction from Form 4562 (not included in Part III)		c	Enter 20% of line 26b subject to limitations (see Instructions)	
13	Dues and publications				
14	Employee benefit programs		d	Subtract line 26c from 26b	
15	Freight (not included in Part III)		27	Utilities and telephone	
16	Insurance		28a	Wages	
17	Interest:		b	Jobs credit	
a	Mortgage (paid to financial institutions)		c	Subtract line 28b from 28a	
b	Other		29	Other expenses (list type and amount):	
18	Laundry and cleaning				
19	Legal and professional services				
20	Office expense				
21	Pension and profit-sharing plans				
22	Rent on business property				

- **30** Add amounts in columns for lines 6 through 29. These are the **total deductions** ▶ | 30 |
- **31** **Net profit or (loss).** Subtract line 30 from line 5. If a profit, enter here and on Form 1040, line 13, and on Schedule SE, line 2 (or line 5 of Form 1041 or Form 1041S). If a loss, you **MUST** go on to line 32 | 31 |
- **32** If you have a loss, you **MUST** answer this question: "Do you have amounts for which you are not at risk in this business?" (See Instructions.) ☐ Yes ☐ No
  If "Yes," you **MUST** attach **Form 6198.** If "No," enter the loss on Form 1040, line 13, and on Schedule SE, line 2 (or line 5 of Form 1041 or Form 1041S).

For Paperwork Reduction Act Notice, see Form 1040 Instructions.   Schedule C (Form 1040) 1987

FORM 1040 - SCHEDULE C, page 2

SAMPLE TAX RETURN FOR SOLE PROPRIETOR

Schedule C (Form 1040) 1987   Page **2**

Part III Cost of Goods Sold and/or Operations (See Schedule C Instructions for Part III)

1. Inventory at beginning of year. (If different from last year's closing inventory, attach explanation.) **1**
2. Purchases less cost of items withdrawn for personal use **2**
3. Cost of labor. (Do not include salary paid to yourself.) **3**
4. Materials and supplies **4**
5. Other costs **5**
6. Add lines 1 through 5 . . . . **6**
7. Less: Inventory at end of year **7**
8. Cost of goods sold and/or operations. Subtract line 7 from line 6. Enter here and in Part I, line 2 . . . . . **8**

Part IV Codes for Principal Business or Professional Activity

Locate the major business category that best describes your activity (for example, Retail Trade, Services, etc.). Within the major category, select the activity code that identifies (or most closely identifies) the business or profession that is the principal source of your sales or receipts. **Enter this 4-digit code on line B on page 1 of Schedule C.** (Note: *If your principal source of income is from farming activities, you should file Schedule F (Form 1040), Farm Income and Expenses.*)

Construction

Code
- 0018 Operative builders (building for own account)

General contractors
- 0034 Residential building
- 0059 Nonresidential building
- 0075 Highway and street construction
- 3889 Other heavy construction (pipe laying, bridge construction, etc.)

Building trade contractors, including repairs
- 0232 Plumbing, heating, air conditioning
- 0257 Painting and paper hanging
- 0273 Electrical work
- 0299 Masonry, dry wall, stone, tile
- 0414 Carpentering and flooring
- 0430 Roofing, siding, and sheet metal
- 0455 Concrete work
- 0471 Water well drilling
- 0885 Other building trade contractors (excavation, glazing, etc.)

Manufacturing, Including Printing and Publishing
- 0612 Bakeries selling at retail
- 0638 Other food products and beverages
- 0653 Textile mill products
- 0679 Apparel and other textile products
- 0695 Leather, footware, handbags, etc.
- 0810 Furniture and fixtures
- 0836 Lumber and other wood products
- 0851 Printing and publishing
- 0877 Paper and allied products
- 0893 Chemicals and allied products
- 1016 Rubber and plastics products
- 1032 Stone, clay, and glass products
- 1057 Primary metal industries
- 1073 Fabricated metal products
- 1099 Machinery and machine shops
- 1115 Electric and electronic equipment
- 1313 Transportation equipment
- 1339 Instruments and related products
- 1883 Other manufacturing industries

Mining and Mineral Extraction
- 1511 Metal mining
- 1537 Coal mining
- 1552 Oil and gas
- 1719 Quarrying and nonmetallic mining

Agricultural Services, Forestry, and Fishing
- 1917 Soil preparation services
- 1933 Crop services
- 1958 Veterinary services, including pets
- 1974 Livestock breeding
- 1990 Other animal services
- 2113 Farm labor and management services
- 2212 Horticulture and landscaping
- 2238 Forestry, except logging
- 0836 Logging
- 2279 Fishing, hunting, and trapping

Wholesale Trade—Selling Goods to Other Businesses, Government, or Institutions, etc.

Durable goods, including machinery, equipment, wood, metals, etc.
- 2618 Selling for your own account

Code
- 2634 Agent or broker for other firms—more than 50% of gross sales on commission

Nondurable goods, including food, fiber, chemicals, etc.
- 2659 Selling for your own account
- 2675 Agent or broker for other firms—more than 50% of gross sales on commission

Retail Trade—Selling Goods to Individuals and Households
- 3012 Selling door-to-door, by telephone or party plan, or from mobile unit
- 3038 Catalog or mail order
- 3053 Vending machine selling

Selling From Store, Showroom, or Other Fixed Location

Food, beverages, and drugs
- 3079 Eating places (meals or snacks)
- 3095 Drinking places (alcoholic beverages)
- 3210 Grocery stores (general line)
- 0612 Bakeries selling at retail
- 3236 Other food stores (meat, produce, candy, etc.)
- 3251 Liquor stores
- 3277 Drug stores

Automotive and service stations
- 3319 New car dealers (franchised)
- 3335 Used car dealers
- 3517 Other automotive dealers (motorcycles, recreational vehicles, etc.)
- 3533 Tires, accessories, and parts
- 3558 Gasoline service stations

General merchandise, apparel, and furniture
- 3715 Variety stores
- 3731 Other general merchandise stores
- 3756 Shoe stores
- 3772 Men's and boys' clothing stores
- 3913 Women's ready-to-wear stores
- 3921 Women's accessory and specialty stores and furriers
- 3939 Family clothing stores
- 3954 Other apparel and accessory stores
- 3970 Furniture stores
- 3996 TV, audio, and electronics
- 3988 Computer and software stores
- 4119 Household appliance stores
- 4317 Other home furnishing stores (china, floor coverings, drapes, etc.)
- 4333 Music and record stores

Building, hardware, and garden supply
- 4416 Building materials dealers
- 4432 Paint, glass, and wallpaper stores
- 4457 Hardware stores
- 4473 Nurseries and garden supply stores

Other retail stores
- 4614 Used merchandise and antique stores (except used motor vehicle parts)
- 4630 Gift, novelty, and souvenir shops
- 4655 Florists
- 4671 Jewelry stores

Code
- 4697 Sporting goods and bicycle shops
- 4812 Boat dealers
- 4838 Hobby, toy, and game shops
- 4853 Camera and photo supply stores
- 4879 Optical goods stores
- 4895 Luggage and leather goods stores
- 5017 Book stores, excluding newsstands
- 5033 Stationery stores
- 5058 Fabric and needlework stores
- 5074 Mobile home dealers
- 5090 Fuel dealers (except gasoline)
- 5884 Other retail stores

Real Estate, Insurance, Finance, and Related Services
- 5512 Real estate agents and managers
- 5538 Operators and lessors of buildings (except developers)
- 5553 Operators and lessors of other real property (except developers)
- 5710 Subdividers and developers, except cemeteries
- 5736 Insurance agents and services
- 5751 Security and commodity brokers, dealers, and investment services
- 5777 Other real estate, insurance, and financial activities

Transportation, Communications, Public Utilities, and Related Services
- 6114 Taxicabs
- 6312 Bus and limousine transportation
- 6338 Trucking (except trash collection)
- 6510 Trash collection without own dump
- 6536 Public warehousing
- 6551 Water transportation
- 6619 Air transportation
- 6635 Travel agents and tour operators
- 6650 Other transportation and related services
- 6676 Communication services
- 6692 Utilities, including dumps, snowplowing, road cleaning, etc.

Services (Providing Personal, Professional, and Business Services)

Hotels and other lodging places
- 7096 Hotels, motels, and tourist homes
- 7211 Rooming and boarding houses
- 7237 Camps and camping parks

Laundry and cleaning services
- 7419 Coin-operated laundries and dry cleaning
- 7435 Other laundry, dry cleaning, and garment services
- 7450 Carpet and upholstery cleaning
- 7476 Janitorial and related services (building, house, and window cleaning)

Business and/or personal services
- 7617 Legal services (or lawyer)
- 7633 Income tax preparation
- 7658 Accounting and bookkeeping
- 7674 Engineering, surveying, and architectural

Code
- 7690 Management, consulting, and public relations
- 7716 Advertising, except direct mail
- 7732 Employment agencies and personnel supply
- 7757 Computer and data processing, including repair and leasing
- 7773 Equipment rental and leasing (except computer or automotive)
- 7914 Investigative and protective services
- 7880 Other business services

Personal services
- 8110 Beauty shops (or beautician)
- 8318 Barber shop (or barber)
- 8334 Photographic portrait studios
- 8516 Shoe repair and shine services
- 8532 Funeral services and crematories
- 8714 Child day care
- 8730 Teaching or tutoring
- 8755 Counseling (except health practitioners)
- 8771 Ministers and chaplains
- 6882 Other personal services

Automotive services
- 8813 Automotive rental or leasing, without driver
- 8839 Parking, except valet
- 8854 General automotive repairs
- 8870 Specialized automotive repairs (brake, body repairs, paint, etc.)
- 8896 Other automotive services (wash, towing, etc.)

Miscellaneous repair, except computers
- 9019 TV and audio equipment repair
- 9035 Other electrical equipment repair
- 9050 Reupholstery and furniture repair
- 2881 Other equipment repair

Medical and health services
- 9217 Offices and clinics of medical doctors (MD's)
- 9233 Offices and clinics of dentists
- 9258 Osteopathic physicians and surgeons
- 9274 Chiropractors
- 9290 Optometrists
- 9415 Registered and practical nurses
- 9431 Other licensed health practitioners
- 9456 Dental laboratories
- 9472 Nursing and personal care facilities
- 9886 Other health services

Amusement and recreational services
- 8557 Physical fitness facilities
- 9613 Videotape rental stores
- 9639 Motion picture theaters
- 9654 Other motion picture and TV film and tape activities
- 9670 Bowling alleys
- 9696 Professional sports and racing, including promoters and managers
- 9811 Theatrical performers, musicians, agents, producers, and related services
- 9837 Other amusement and recreational services

- 8888 Unable to classify

Keeping Records   115

FORM 1040 - SCHEDULE SE

SELF-EMPLOYMENT TAX COMPUTATION SAMPLE

SCHEDULE SE (Form 1040)
Department of the Treasury
Internal Revenue Service (3)

Computation of Social Security Self-Employment Tax
► See Instructions for Schedule SE (Form 1040).
► Attach to Form 1040.

OMB No. 1545-0074
1987
Attachment Sequence No. 18

Name of person with **self-employment** income (as shown on social security card) | Social security number of person with **self-employment** income ►

A If your only self-employment income was from earnings as a minister, member of a religious order, or Christian Science practitioner, AND you filed Form 4361, then DO NOT file Schedule SE. Instead, write "Exempt-Form 4361" on Form 1040, line 48. However, if you filed Form 4361, but have $400 or more of other earnings subject to self-employment tax, continue with Part I and check here ► ☐

B If you filed Form 4029 and have received IRS approval, DO NOT file Schedule SE. Write "Exempt-Form 4029" on Form 1040, line 48.

C If your only earnings subject to self-employment tax are wages from an electing church or church-controlled organization that is exempt from employer social security taxes and you are not a minister or a member of a religious order, skip lines 1–8. Enter zero on line 9. Continue with line 11a.

Part I — Regular Computation of Net Earnings From Self-Employment

1. Net farm profit (or loss) from Schedule F (Form 1040), line 37, and farm partnerships, Schedule K-1 (Form 1065), line 14a **1**
2. Net profit (or loss) from Schedule C (Form 1040), line 31, and Schedule K-1 (Form 1065), line 14a (other than farming). (See Instructions for other income to report.) Employees of an electing church or church-controlled organization DO NOT enter your Form W-2 wages on line 2. See the Instructions ... **2**

Part II — Optional Computation of Net Earnings From Self-Employment (See "Who Can Use Schedule SE" in the Instructions.)

See Instructions for limitations. Generally, this part may be used **only** if you meet any of the following tests:

A Your **gross** farm income[1] was not more than $2,400; or
B Your **gross** farm income[1] was more than $2,400 and your **net** farm profits[2] were **less** than $1,600; or
C Your **net** nonfarm profits[3] were less than $1,600 and your **net** nonfarm profits[3] were also **less** than two-thirds (⅔) of your **gross** nonfarm income.[4]

Note: *If line 2 above is two-thirds (⅔) or more of your gross nonfarm income[4], or, if line 2 is $1,600 or more, you may not use the optional method.*

[1]From Schedule F (Form 1040), line 12, and Schedule K-1 (Form 1065), line 14b.   [3]From Schedule C (Form 1040), line 31, and Schedule K-1 (Form 1065), line 14a.
[2]From Schedule F (Form 1040), line 37, and Schedule K-1 (Form 1065), line 14a.   [4]From Schedule C (Form 1040), line 5, and Schedule K-1 (Form 1065), line 14c.

3. Maximum income for optional methods .... **3** | $1,600 | 00
4. Farm Optional Method—If you meet test A or B above, enter the **smaller of:** two-thirds (⅔) of gross farm income from Schedule F (Form 1040), line 12, and farm partnerships, Schedule K-1 (Form 1065), line 14b; **or $1,600** **4**
5. Subtract line 4 from line 3 .... **5**
6. Nonfarm Optional Method—If you meet test C above, enter the **smallest of:** two-thirds (⅔) of gross nonfarm income from Schedule C (Form 1040), line 5, and Schedule K-1 (Form 1065), line 14c (other than farming); **or $1,600; or,** if you elected the farm optional method, the amount on line 5 ..... **6**

Part III — Computation of Social Security Self-Employment Tax

7. Enter the amount from Part I, line 1, **or,** if you elected the farm optional method, Part II, line 4 .... **7**
8. Enter the amount from Part I, line 2, **or,** if you elected the nonfarm optional method, Part II, line 6 .... **8**
9. Add lines 7 and 8. If less than $400, do not file this schedule. (Exception: If you are an employee of an electing church or church-controlled organization and the total of lines 7 and 8 is less than $400, enter zero and complete the rest of this schedule.) **9**
10. The largest amount of combined wages and self-employment earnings subject to social security or railroad retirement tax (tier 1) for 1987 is .... **10** | $43,800 | 00
11a. Total social security wages and tips from Forms W-2 and railroad retirement compensation (tier 1). **Note:** *Medicare qualified government employees whose wages are only subject to the 1.45% medicare (hospital insurance benefits) tax and employees of certain church or church-controlled organizations should not include those wages on this line. (See Instructions.)* **11a**
   b. Unreported tips subject to social security tax from Form 4137, line 9, or to railroad retirement tax (tier 1) **11b**
   c. Add lines 11a and 11b **11c**
12a. Subtract line 11c from line 10. (If zero or less, enter zero.) **12a**
   b. Enter your medicare qualified government wages if you are required to use the worksheet in Part III of the Instructions **12b**
   c. Enter your Form W-2 wages of $100 or more from an electing church or church-controlled organization **12c**
   d. Add lines 9 and 12c **12d**
13. Enter the smaller of line 12a or line 12d **13**
    If line 13 is $43,800, enter $5,387.40 on line 14. Otherwise, multiply line 13 by .123 and enter the result on line 14 .... x .123
14. Self-employment tax. Enter this amount on Form 1040, line 48 .... **14**

For Paperwork Reduction Act Notice, see Form 1040 Instructions.   Schedule SE (Form 1040) 1987

FORM 4562

DEPRECIATION SCHEDULE SAMPLE

Form 4562 | **Depreciation and Amortization** | OMB No. 1545-0172
Department of the Treasury | ▶ See separate instructions. | **1987**
Internal Revenue Service (3) | ▶ Attach this form to your return. | Attachment Sequence No. 67

Name(s) as shown on return | Identifying number

Business or activity to which this form relates

Part I Depreciation (Do not use this part for automobiles, certain other vehicles, computers, and property used for entertainment, recreation, or amusement. Instead, use Part III.)

Section A.—Election To Expense Depreciable Assets Placed In Service During This Tax Year (Section 179)

(a) Description of property	(b) Date placed in service	(c) Cost	(d) Expense deduction
1			

2 Listed property—Enter total from Part III, Section A, column (h) . . . .
3 Total (add lines 1 and 2, but do not enter more than $10,000) . . . .
4 Enter the amount, if any, by which the cost of all section 179 property placed in service during this tax year is more than $200,000 . . . .
5 Subtract line 4 from line 3. If result is less than zero, enter zero. (See instructions for other limitations) . .

Section B.—Depreciation

(a) Class of property	(b) Date placed in service	(c) Basis for depreciation (Business use only—see instructions)	(d) Recovery period	(e) Method of figuring depreciation	(f) Deduction
6 Accelerated Cost Recovery System (ACRS) (see instructions): *For assets placed in service ONLY during tax year beginning in 1987*					
a 3-year property					
b 5-year property					
c 7-year property					
d 10-year property					
e 15-year property					
f 20-year property					
g Residential rental property					
h Nonresidential real property					

7 Listed property—Enter total from Part III, Section A, column (g) . . . .
8 ACRS deduction for assets placed in service prior to 1987 (see instructions) . . . .

Section C.—Other Depreciation

9 Property subject to section 168(f)(1) election (see instructions) . . . .
10 Other depreciation (see instructions) . . . .

Section D.—Summary

11 Total (add deductions on lines 5 through 10). Enter here and on the Depreciation line of your return (Partnerships and S corporations—Do NOT include any amounts entered on line 5.) . . . .
12 For assets above placed in service during the current year, enter the portion of the basis attributable to additional section 263A costs. (See instructions for who must use.) . .

Part II Amortization

(a) Description of property	(b) Date acquired	(c) Cost or other basis	(d) Code section	(e) Amortization period or percentage	(f) Amortization for this year
1 Amortization for property placed in service **only** during tax year beginning in 1987					
2 Amortization for property placed in service prior to 1987					

3 Total. Enter here and on Other Deductions or Other Expenses line of your return . . . .

See Paperwork Reduction Act Notice on page 1 of the separate instructions.   Form **4562** (1987)

Keeping Records

FORM 4562

DEPRECIATION SCHEDULE SAMPLE - page 2

Form 4562 (1987) — Page 2

Part III — Automobiles, Certain Other Vehicles, Computers, and Property Used for Entertainment, Recreation, or Amusement (Listed Property).

If you are using the standard mileage rate or deducting vehicle lease expense, complete columns (a) through (d) of Section A, all of Section B, and Section C if applicable.

Section A.—Depreciation (If automobiles and other listed property placed in service after June 18, 1984, are used 50% or less in a trade or business, the Section 179 deduction is not allowed and depreciation must be taken using the straight line method over 5 years. For other limitations, see instructions.)

Do you have evidence to support the business use claimed? ☐ Yes ☐ No   If yes, is the evidence written? ☐ Yes ☐ No

(a) Type of property (list vehicles first)	(b) Date placed in service	(c) Business use percentage (%)	(d) Cost or other basis (see instructions for leased property)	(e) Basis for depreciation (Business use only—see instructions)	(f) Depreciation method and recovery period	(g) Depreciation deduction	(h) Section 179 expense

Total (Enter here and on line 2, page 1.) . . . .

Total (Enter here and on line 7, page 1.) . . . .

Section B.—Information Regarding Use of Vehicles

Complete this section as follows, if you deduct expenses for vehicles:
- Always complete this section for vehicles used by a sole proprietor, partner, or other more than 5% owner or related person.
- If you provided vehicles to employees, first answer the questions in Section C to see if you meet an exception to completing this section for those items.

	Vehicle 1	Vehicle 2	Vehicle 3	Vehicle 4	Vehicle 5	Vehicle 6
1 Total miles driven during the year . . .						
2 Total business miles driven during the year						
3 Total commuting miles driven during the year.						
4 Total other personal (noncommuting) miles driven						

	Yes	No	Yes	No	Yes	No	Yes	No	Yes	No	Yes	No
5 Was the vehicle available for personal use during off-duty hours?												
6 Was the vehicle used primarily by a more than 5% owner or related person? . . .												
7 Is another vehicle available for personal use? . .												

Section C.—Questions for Employers Who Provide Vehicles for Use by Employees.
(Answer these questions to determine if you meet an exception to completing Section B. Note: Section B must always be completed for vehicles used by sole proprietors, partners, or other more than 5% owners or related persons.)

	Yes	No
8 Do you maintain a written policy statement that prohibits all personal use of vehicles, including commuting, by your employees?		
9 Do you maintain a written policy statement that prohibits personal use of vehicles, except commuting, by your employees? (See instructions for vehicles used by corporate officers, directors, or 1% or more owners.)		
10 Do you treat all use of vehicles by employees as personal use?		
11 Do you provide more than five vehicles to your employees and retain the information received from your employees concerning the use of the vehicles?		
12 Do you meet the requirements concerning fleet vehicles or qualified automobile demonstration use (see instructions)?		

Note: *If your answer to 8, 9, 10, 11, or 12 is "Yes," you need not complete Section B for the covered vehicles.*

RECORDS RETENTION
SUGGESTED SCHEDULE

RETENTION PERIOD	AUTHORITY TO DISPOSE
1-10 - No. Years to be Retained PR - Retain Permanently EOY - Retain Until End of Year CJ - Retain Until Completion of Job EXP - Retain Until Expiration ED - Retain Until Equipment Disposal	AD - Administrative Decision FLSA - Fair Labor Standards Act CFR - Code of Federal Regulations IR - Insurance Regulation

TYPE OF RECORD	RETAIN FOR	BY WHOSE AUTHORITY
BANK DEPOSIT RECORDS	7	AD
BANK STATEMENTS	7	AD
BUSINESS LICENSES	EXP	AD
CATALOGS	EXP	AD
CHECK REGISTER	PR	AD
CHECKS (CANCELLED)	3	FLSA, STATE
CONTRACTS	EXP	AD
CORRESPONDENCE	5	AD
DEPRECIATION RECORDS	PR	CFR
ESTIMATED TAX RECORDS	PR	AD
EXPENSE RECORDS	7	AD
INSURANCE (CLAIMS RECORDS)	11	IR
INSURANCE POLICIES	EXP	AD
INVENTORY RECORD	10	AD
INVENTORY REPORTS	PR	CFR
INVOICES (ACCT. PAYABLE)	3	FLSA, STATE
INVOICES (ACCT. RECEIVABLE)	7	AD
LEDGER (GENERAL)	PR	CFR
MAINTENANCE RECORDS	ED	AD
OFFICE EQUIPMENT RECORDS	5	AD
PATENTS	PR	AD
PETTY CASH RECORD	PR	AD
POSTAL RECORDS	1	AD, CFR
PURCHASE ORDERS	3	CFR
SALES TAX REPORTS TO STATE	PR	STATE
SHIPPING DOCUMENTS	2-10	AD, CFR
TAX BILLS & STATEMENTS	PR	AD
TAX RETURNS (FED. & STATE)	PR	AD
TRADEMARKS & COPYRIGHTS	PR	AD
TRAVEL RECORDS	7	AD
WORK PAPERS (PROJECTS)	CJ	AD
YEAR-END REPORTS	PR	AD

Keeping Records

GENERAL JOURNAL
Sample Page

CHECK #	DATE	TRANSACTION	CREDIT	DEBIT	SALES	S. TAX	REPAIRS	PURCH.	ADVERT.	MISCELL.
		Balance forward--	326 00							
234	7/13	J.J. Advertising		172 56	100 00	6 00	220 00	62 00	63 56	47 00
235	7/13	Rutger Products		32 00					32 00	
236	7/16	Regal Stationers		51 00				51 00		
***	7/17	SALES Taylor	81 70	23 42	45 00	2 70				23 42
***	7/17	Jones			34 00 RESALE					
237	7/19	REPAIRS Davis $20, Jones $35, Smith $85	140 00				140 00			
		PETTY CASH DEPOSIT		50 00						50 00
		TOTALS	547 70	328 98	179 00	8 70	360 00	113 00	95 56	120 42

120

OUT OF YOUR MIND AND INTO THE MARKETPLACE

PROFIT AND LOSS SHEET
1 9 8 ___

	RECEIPTS	DISBURSE	MON. BAL	YTD RECEIPTS	YTD DISPURSE.	YTD BALANCE
JANUARY						
FEBRUARY						
MARCH						
APRIL						
MAY						
JUNE						
JULY						
AUGUST						
SEPTEMBER						
OCTOBER						
NOVEMBER						
DECEMBER						
TOTALS						

NOTE: YTD = Year To Date

A. **END OF EACH MONTH** - Enter totals from General Journal.
B. **END OF YEAR** - Compute final totals for year' overview.
C. **USE IN SUCCEEDING YEARS** - Excellent for seeing trends.

Keeping Records

PETTY CASH RECORD

DATE	REASON FOR DEBIT	DEPOSIT	EXPENSE	BALANCE

NOTE: 1. Save all receipts for cash purchases!!!!
2. Record purchases WEEKLY in Petty Cash Record.
3. File all receipts. These are deductible.
4. Be sure to record your Petty Cash deposits.

INVENTORY RECORD

DATE PURCH.	ITEM PURCHASED (description and stock no.)	PURCH. PRICE	BUYER'S NAME	SALE DATE	SALE PRICE	SALES TAX

NOTE: The Inventory Record shown above is to be used for keeping track of items purchased for resale. Each page should deal with only one category. If you buy from several companies, you might use each company's name as a heading. This will make the information easy to retrieve when it is needed. Inventories for tools, equipment, etc. do not need the last four columns.

KEEP YOUR INVENTORY CURRENT!

Keeping Records

TRAVEL RECORD

DATE	LOCATION	REASON FOR EXPENSE	NO. MILES	COST OF EXPENSE

NOTE: 1. Mileage records are required by the IRS.
2. If you take a business trip, keep all of your receipts in one folder. You should keep your travel log with you and record expenses as they occur. Trip records are impossible to remember after the fact!!!

SUMMARY OF REVENUE AND EXPENSES

MONTH	DEBIT	CREDIT	INT	REPAIR	SALES	S.TAX	RESALE ITEMS	SUPP.	TOOLS	FREIGHT	ADVERT	TELE	CONTRAC. SERV.	AUTO	MISC
JANUARY															
FEBRUARY															
MARCH															
APRIL															
MAY															
JUNE															
JULY															
AUGUST															
SEPTEMBER															
OCTOBER															
NOVEMBER															
DECEMBER															
TOTALS															

BEGINNING INVENTORY (Jan. 1) $ _____
ENDING INVENTORY (Dec. 31) $ _____

FED. INCOME TAX PAID FOR 198__ $ _____
STATE INCOME TAX PD. FOR 198__ $ _____

Keeping Records

Company Name
BALANCE SHEET
_____ ____, 19____

ASSETS

Current Assets
- Cash $_____
- Petty Cash $_____
- Accounts Receivable $_____
- Inventory $_____
- Short-Term Investments $_____
- Prepaid Expenses $_____

Long-Term Investments $_____

Fixed Assets
- Land $_____
- Buildings $_____
- Improvements $_____
- Equipment $_____
- Furniture $_____
- Autos/Vehicles $_____

Other Assets
1. $_____
2. $_____
3. $_____
4. $_____

TOTAL ASSETS $_____

LIABILITIES

Current Liabilities
- Accounts Payable $_____
- Notes Payable $_____
- Interest Payable $_____
- Taxes Payable
  - Fed. Inc. Tax $_____
  - State Inc. Tax $_____
  - Self-Emp. Tax $_____
  - Sales Tax (SBE) $_____
  - Property Tax $_____
- Payroll Accrual $_____

Long-Term Liabilities
- Notes Payable $_____

TOTAL LIABILITIES $_____

NET WORTH

Proprietorship $_____
or
Partnership
- (Name's) Equity $_____
- (Name's) Equity $_____
or
Corporation
- Capital Stock $_____
- Surplus Paid In $_____
- Retained Earnings $_____

TOTAL NET WORTH $_____

Assets - Liabilities = Net Worth

Total Liabilities and Equity will <u>always</u> be equal to Total Assets!

OUT OF YOUR MIND AND INTO THE MARKETPLACE

BALANCE SHEET

(Explanation of Categories on Balance Sheet)

I. ASSETS - Everything owned by or owed to the business that has cash value

   A. Current Assets - Assets that can be converted into cash within one year of the date on the Balance Sheet
   1. **Cash** - Money you have on hand. Include monies not yet deposited.
   2. **Petty Cash** - Money deposited to Petty Cash & not yet expended.
   3. **Accounts Receivable** - Money owed to you for goods and/or services
   4. **Inventory** - Raw materials, work in process and goods manufactured or purchased for resale.
   5. **Short-Term Investments** - (Expected to be converted to cash within one year) Stocks, bonds, C.D.'s. List at the lesser of cost or market value.
   6. **Prepaid Expenses** - Goods/services purchased or rented priod to use.

   B. Long-Term Investments - Stocks, bonds, and special savings accounts to be kept for at least one year.

   C. Fixed Assets - The resources a business owns and does not intend for resale.
   1. **Land** - List at original purchase price.
   2. **Buildings** - List at cost less depreciation.
   3. **Equipment, Furniture, Autos/Vehicles** - List at cost less depreciation. Kelley Blue Book can be used to determine value of autos/vehicles.

   D. Other Assets - Any assets not listed above. List separately and value in terms of current worth.

II. LIABILITIES - What your business owes; claims by creditors on your assets.

   A. Current Liabilities - Obligations payable within one operating cycle
   1. **Accounts Payable** - Amounts owed by you for goods or services.
   2. **Notes Payable** - Short-term notes, list the balance of principal due. Separately list the current portion of long-term notes.
   3. **Interest Payable** - Interst accrued on loans and credit.
   4. **Taxes Payable** - Amounts estimated to have been incurred during accounting period.
   5. **Payroll Accrual** - Current Liabilities on salaries and wages.

   B. Long-Term Liabilities - Outstanding balance less current portion due. (Ex. - Mortgage)

III. NET WORTH - Also called "EQUITY" - The claims of the owner or owners on the assets of the business.

   A. Proprietorship or Partnership - each owner's original investment plus earnings after withdrawels.
   B. Corporation - The sum or contributions by owners or stockholders plus earnings retained after paying dividends.

Keeping Records

INCOME STATEMENT
(Also Known AS: Profit & Loss Statement)

THE INCOME STATEMENT - is compiled from actual business transactions, in contrast to the Pro Forma Cash Flow Statement, which is a projection for a future business period. It is one of the two principle financial statements prepared from the ledgers and the records of a business. At the end of each fiscal period, accounts are balanced and closed. **Income and Expense Account Balances** are transferred to the Summary of Revenue and Expenses and are then used in the Income Statement. The remaining Asset, Liability, and Capital information derived from your records provides the figures for the Balance Sheet which has already been covered earlier in this section of the book.

The Statement of Income - shows where your money has come from and where it was spent over a specific period of time. It is an excellent way to measure a company's income from sales or services. It must be prepared not only at the end of the fiscal year, but at the close of each business month. This will give you a picture of the results of your operations for the previous period

FORMAT - INCOME STATEMENT

1. **INCOME**
   a. Net Sales - gross sales less returns & allowances.
   b. Cost of Goods Sold - see Form 1040, Sched. C for computation.
   c. Gross Profit on Sales - Net Sales less Cost of Goods Sold.

2. **EXPENSES**
   a. Selling (Direct or Controllable) - related to product or service.
   b. Administrative (Indirect or Fixed) - Not product related.

3. **INCOME FROM OPERATIONS** - Income less Expenses.

4. **OTHER INCOME** - Interest, etc.

5. **OTHER EXPENSE** - Interest expense, etc.

6. **NET PROFIT (LOSS) BEFORE TAXES**

7. **TAXES**

8. **NET PROFIT (LOSS) AFTER TAXES**

An example of an INCOME STATEMENT can be found on the following page.

INCOME STATEMENT
(Also Called: Profit & Loss Statement)

For the Period Beginning_____and Ending_____.

INCOME
1. NET SALES (Gross - Ret. & Allow.)
2. Cost of Goods Sold
   a. Inventory (January 1st)
   b. Purchases
   c. Cost of goods avail. for sale (a.+b.)
   d. Deduct Inventory December 31st
3. GROSS PROFIT ON SALES

EXPENSES
1. Selling Expense (Direct or Controllable)
   a. Advertising
   b. Freight
   c. Legal Fees
   d. Packaging Costs
   e. Parts & Supplies
   f. Sales Salaries
   g. Miscellaneous Direct Expenses
2. Administrative Expense (Indirect, Fixed)
   a. Depreciation Expense
   b. Insurance
   c. Licenses & Permits
   d. Office Salaries
   e. Rent Expense
   f. Taxes & Licenses
   g. Utilities
   h. Miscellaneous Indirect Expenses

TOTAL EXPENSES

INCOME FROM OPERATIONS (Inc. less Exp.)

OTHER INCOME
1. Interest Income

OTHER EXPENSE
1. Interest Expense

NET PROFIT (LOSS) BEFORE INCOME TAXES

INCOME TAXES

NET PROFIT (LOSS) AFTER INCOME TAXES

Keeping Records

IRS FORMS & PUBLICATIONS
HOW TO ORDER FREE INFORMATION

How To Get Forms

Generally, we mail forms and schedules directly to you based on what seems to be right for you. Schedules and forms you may need are listed below. Also see list of related publications.

You can order the following items from IRS or get them at many participating banks, post offices, or libraries:

- **Form 1040,** U.S. Individual Income Tax Return
- Instructions for Form 1040
- **Form 1040A**
- Instructions for Form 1040A
- **Form 1040EZ**
- Instructions for Form 1040EZ
- **Schedule A** for itemized deductions
- **Schedule B** for interest income if more than $400; for dividends and other distributions on stock if more than $400; and for answering the Foreign Accounts or Foreign Trusts questions

You can photocopy the following items (as well as those listed above) at many participating libraries or order them from IRS:

- **Schedule C,** Profit or (Loss) From Business or Profession
- **Schedule D,** Capital Gains and Losses and Reconciliation of Forms 1099-B
- **Schedule E,** Supplemental Income Schedule
- **Schedule F,** Farm Income and Expenses
- **Schedule R,** Credit for the Elderly or for the Permanently and Totally Disabled
- **Schedule SE,** Computation of Social Security Self-Employment Tax
- **Form 1040-ES,** Estimated Tax for Individuals
- **Form 2106,** Employee Business Expenses
- **Form 2119,** Sale or Exchange of Principal Residence
- **Form 2210,** Underpayment of Estimated Tax by Individuals
- **Form 2441,** Credit for Child and Dependent Care Expenses
- **Form 3468,** Computation of Investment Credit
- **Form 3903,** Moving Expenses
- **Form 4136,** Computation of Credit for Federal Tax on Gasoline and Special Fuels
- **Form 4562,** Depreciation and Amortization
- **Form 4684,** Casualties and Thefts
- **Form 4797,** Gains and Losses From Sales or Exchanges of Assets Used in a Trade or Business and Involuntary Conversions
- **Form 4868,** Application for Automatic Extension of Time To File U.S. Individual Income Tax Return
- **Form 5695,** Residential Energy Credit Carryforward
- **Form 6251,** Alternative Minimum Tax-Individuals
- **Form 8283,** Noncash Charitable Contributions
- **Form 8332,** Release of Claim to Exemption for Child of Divorced or Separated Parents
- **Form 8582,** Passive Activity Loss Limitations
- **Form 8598,** Home Mortgage Interest
- **Form 8606,** Nondeductible IRA Contributions, IRA Basis, and Nontaxable IRA Distributions
- **Form 8615,** Computation of Tax for Children Under Age 14 Who Have Investment Income of More Than $1,000

How To Get Publications

The following publications can be ordered from IRS or you can read or photocopy them at many participating libraries:

- 17 Your Federal Income Tax
- 54 Tax Guide for U.S. Citizens and Resident Aliens Abroad
- 334 Tax Guide for Small Business
- 463 Travel, Entertainment, and Gift Expenses
- 501 Exemptions and Standard Deduction
- 502 Medical and Dental Expenses
- 503 Child and Dependent Care Credit, and Employment Taxes for Household Employers
- 504 Tax Information for Divorced or Separated Individuals
- 505 Tax Withholding and Estimated Tax
- 508 Educational Expenses
- 521 Moving Expenses
- 523 Tax Information on Selling Your Home
- 524 Credit for the Elderly or for the Permanently and Totally Disabled
- 525 Taxable and Nontaxable Income
- 526 Charitable Contributions
- 527 Rental Property
- 529 Miscellaneous Deductions
- 530 Tax Information for Owners of Homes, Condominiums, and Cooperative Apartments
- 531 Reporting Income From Tips
- 533 Self-Employment Tax
- 545 Interest Expense
- 547 Nonbusiness Disasters, Casualties, and Thefts
- 550 Investment Income and Expenses
- 552 Recordkeeping for Individuals and a List of Tax Publications
- 553 Highlights of 1987 Tax Changes
- 554 Tax Information for Older Americans
- 575 Pension and Annuity Income
- 583 Information for Business Taxpayers
- 587 Business Use of Your Home
- 590 Individual Retirement Arrangements (IRAs)
- 596 Earned Income Credit
- 907 Tax Information for Handicapped and Disabled Individuals
- 910 Guide to Free Tax Services
- 915 Social Security Benefits and Equivalent Railroad Retirement Benefits
- 917 Business Use of a Car
- 920 Explanation of the Tax Reform Act of 1986 for Individuals
- 921 Explanation of the Tax Reform Act of 1986 for Business
- 929 Tax Rules for Children and Dependents

Other publications and forms referred to in the instructions are also available without cost from the "Forms Distribution Center" for your state. See Publication 910 for a complete list of available publications.

Where To Send Your Order for Free Forms and Publications

If you are located in:	Send to "Forms Distribution Center" for your state
Alaska, Arizona, California, Colorado, Hawaii, Idaho, Montana, Nevada, New Mexico, Oregon, Utah, Washington, Wyoming	P.O. Box 12626, Fresno, CA 93778
Alabama, Arkansas, Illinois, Indiana, Iowa, Kansas, Kentucky, Louisiana, Michigan, Minnesota, Mississippi, Missouri, Nebraska, North Dakota, Ohio, Oklahoma, South Dakota, Tennessee, Texas, Wisconsin	P.O. Box 9903, Bloomington, IL 61799
Connecticut, Delaware, District of Columbia, Florida, Georgia, Maine, Maryland, Massachusetts, New Hampshire, New Jersey, New York, North Carolina, Pennsylvania, Rhode Island, South Carolina, Vermont, Virginia, West Virginia	P.O. Box 25866, Richmond, VA 23260

Foreign Addresses—Taxpayers with mailing addresses in foreign countries should send this order blank to either: Forms Distribution Center, P.O. Box 25866, Richmond, VA 23260; or Forms Distribution Center, P.O. Box 12626, Fresno, CA 93778, whichever is closer. Send letter requests for other forms and publications to: Forms Distribution Center, P.O. Box 25866, Richmond, VA 23260.

Puerto Rico—Forms Distribution Center, P.O. Box 25866, Richmond, VA 23260

Virgin Islands—V.I. Bureau of Internal Revenue, P.O. Box 3186, St. Thomas, VI 00801

Detach at this Line

Order Blank—We will send you 2 copies of each form and 1 copy of each set of instructions or publication you circle. Please cut the order blank on the dotted line and be sure to print or type your name and address accurately on the other side. This will be the label used to return material to you. Enclose this order blank in your own envelope and address your envelope to the IRS address shown above for your state. To help reduce waste, please order only the forms and publications you think you will need to prepare your return. Use the blank spaces to order items not listed. If you need more space, attach a separate sheet of paper listing the additional forms and publications you may need. Be sure to allow 2 weeks to receive your order.

The items printed in blue may be picked up at many banks, post offices, and libraries. (3)

Circle Desired Forms and Publications							
		Schedule SE (1040)	4136	8598 & Instructions	Pub. 503	Pub. 527	Pub. 920
		1040-ES (1988)	4562 & Instructions	8606	Pub. 504	Pub. 529	Pub. 921
1040	Schedules A&B (1040)	2106 & Instructions	4684 & Instructions	8615	Pub. 505	Pub. 530	Pub. 929
Instructions for 1040 & Schedules	Schedule C (1040)	2119	4797 & Instructions	Pub. 17	Pub. 508	Pub. 545	
1040A	Schedule D (1040)	2210 & Instructions	4868	Pub. 334	Pub. 521	Pub. 552	
1040EZ	Schedule E (1040)	2441	6251 & Instructions	Pub. 463	Pub. 523	Pub. 553	
1040A & 1040EZ Instructions	Schedule F (1040)	3468 & Instructions	8283 & Instructions	Pub. 501	Pub. 524	Pub. 554	
1040X & Instructions	Schedule R (1040) & Instructions	3903 & Instructions	8582 & Instructions	Pub. 502	Pub. 526	Pub. 917	

Page 49

Keeping Records

GENERAL RECORDKEEPING SCHEDULE

1. DAILY
   a. File mail in appropriate folders.
   b. Record inventory information as shipments are received.
   c. Pay any invoices necessary to meet discount deadlines.

2. WEEKLY
   a. Prepare deposit.
   b. Enter deposit in ledger and checkbook.
   c. Enter week's checking transactions in General Ledger
   d. Enter sales information in Inventory Record.
   e. Record petty cash purchases and file receipts.
   f. Pay invoices due. Be aware of discount dates.
   g. Enter items purchased in appropriate records. (ex.- tools, office equip.)

3. MONTHLY
   a. Balance checkbook (Reconcile w/statement).
   b. Enter any interest earned and any bank charges in General Ledger and Checkbook.
   c. Total and balance all ledger columns.
   d. Enter totals of receipts and disbursements on Profit & Loss Sheet.

4. QUARTERLY
   a. File Estimated Taxes with the Internal Revenue Service and the State.

   Due Dates: April 15th
              June 15th
              Sept. 15th
              January 15th

   Note: There are only two months between the 1st and 2nd Quarters. There are four months between the 3rd and 4th Quarter filing deadlines.

   b. Fill out and send in your sales tax report to the State Board of Equalization (with a check for monies collected for sales tax).

   Note: The SBE may require you to file either quarterly or annually.

OUT OF YOUR MIND AND INTO THE MARKETPLACE

GENERAL RECORDKEEPING SCHEDULE

page 2

5. **ANNUALLY**
   a. Transfer all monthly totals from the General Ledger to the Summary of Revenue and Expenses.
   b. Prepare a Balance Sheet if appropriate.
   c. Schedule appointment with your accountant. Do not wait until he is pressed for time.
   d. Send out 1099's and 599's to independent contractors. They are due January 31st for the previous tax year.
   e. Set up your books for the new year.
   f. Retrieve all tax information needed for income tax returns.

   Note: Use the tax forms appropriate for your business to determine what information you need.

   g. File your sales tax with the State Board of Equalization.
   h. File all records and pertinent material for the tax year in one place.

IMPORTANT: It is important that you keep in mind that there may be recordkeeping responsibilites not noted in this schedule. Each business has different requirements. Be aware of your requirements. Talk to an accountant and to others in your type of business. They will be able to give you information that will not only make your year more profitable, but also one in which your recordkeeping will work for you. **A SUCCESSFUL BUSINESS MUST HAVE ACCURATE RECORDS!**

Keeping Records

13.

SELECTING YOUR INSURANCE

13. SELECTING YOUR INSURANCE

At some point during the formation of a small or home-based business, the question of insurance needs will necessarily arise. Today's world of rapidly-expanding technology goes hand-in-hand with a society steeped in lawsuits. The most innocent business owner can find himself involved in legal actions against his business while in the pursuit of his affairs. If you are going to carry on with your business and feel secure, it will be necessary for you to obtain insurance, especially if you are a home-based business. In fact, the cost for your particular insurance needs may be prohibitive. At this point, you must determine whether or not the risks involved are worth taking. If you choose not to insure yourself, you may wish to form your business under the corporate structure in order to separate your business and personal assets. Either way, the question of insurance requires careful consideration.

SHOPPING FOR AN INSURANCE COMPANY

Shopping for an insurance company is like shopping for a bank. Careful research will help you to determine what company can best serve your needs and still be within the realm of practicality. Many times, business insurance companies will advertise in trade journals, especially if that type of insurance is not available with major companies. For instance, food industries must usually seek a specialized insurance company. Consider your specific needs before shopping. The following page contains information which may help you to select your business insurance. We have purposely touched lightly on the matter of insurance. Only you can make the final decision as to whether or not you want to purchase insurance and, if so, what limits will leave you feeling comfortable and secure.

INSURANCE FACT SHEET

I. **TYPES OF BUSINESS INSURANCE**

    A. CASUALTY
        General Liability
        Specific Liability Coverage
        Fire
        Theft
        Workman's Compensation
        Business Interruption Insurance

    B. LIFE
        Life Insurance
        Disability Insurance
        Employee Benefits
        Group Insurance
        Retirement Programs
        Overhead Expense

II. **FIGURE OUT YOUR INSURANCE PRIORITY SHOPPING LIST**

    A. Immediate Protection that is:
        1. Required_____
        2. Necessary_____
        3. Desirable_____

    B. Long-Term Protection that is:
        1. Essential_____
        2. Necessary_____
        3. Required_____

III. **KEY POINTS**

    A. Insurance is and should be a major factor to consider in forming a business.

    B. First year casualty premiums will sometimes be higher than other years due to frequency of misstatement by the insured and high risk to the insurance company.

    C. Choosing your insurance agent/broker (consultant and buyer) is one of the most important decisions you can make.

IV. **FIVE STEPS TO PREVENT YOUR BUSINESS FROM FAILING BY AN "INSURABLE" CAUSE.**

    A. Recognize risks you will be facing.

    B. Follow guidelines for covering them economically.

    C. Have a plan in mind.

    D. Get advice from experts.

    E. Do it!

Selecting Your Insurance

14. MARKETING YOUR BUSINESS

14. MARKETING YOUR BUSINESS

The development of a good marketing plan is essential to your business development. Your product or service may be in demand and your pricing competitive. You may have found the lowest prices for your raw materials and may have secured adequate financing for your business. All of these will be of no use if you have not taken the time to identify your customers and found the means to get your product to them. The key word here is **time**. It takes time to research and develop a marketing plan, but it is time well spent.

There are professional level firms and individual consultants who can conduct market research for you. They conduct market surveys, compile the data, and make recommendations. This may be too costly for the small or home-based business. Don't overlook non-professional sources of help. Students generally are an inexpensive labor pool for conducting surveys. Also contact the Business Departments of colleges and universities in your area. Their students majoring in Marketing may need a project and your business could fill that need.

You may choose to do your own market survey. Most of the information you need can be found in your public library and in the publications of the Department of Commerce, the Small Business Administration and the Census Bureau. By doing your own marketing research and developing your own plan, you will have demystified marketing. You will learn all there is to know about your type of business.

So far, your focus has been as a salesperson with a concern for you product or service. A person concerned with marketing must be consumer-oriented. You must change your focus. Try to be objective and try to think like your customers. If you have decided to conduct your own **MARKET RESEARCH**, outline your objectives. You want to **survey the market, check out the competition,** and **identify your target market.** Once you have identified your target market (your customers), you can develop your **MARKETING PLAN.** Your plan will include **packaging design, pricing, advertising, distribution,** and **timing of market entry.**

MARKET RESEARCH

Market research takes careful planning. Keep a record of all of your findings. Worksheet samples are included at the end of this section to help you in your research.

SURVEY THE MARKET

At this point, you are not concerned with identifying your customer. You are surveying the market in a general way. You want to know if a need exists for your product or service. Will the customer have an interest in what you have to offer? Market research involves finding out what a customer wants and needs and determining how your business can meet those wants and needs. Don't underestimate personal observation. Watch current buying trends. You can learn a great deal about the buying habits of your area by watching the purchases in the supermarket check-out lines as well as at the stores in the mall. Listen to friends. What products or services do they wish were available?

Surveys are an excellent means of determining the response to what you have to offer. A questionnaire is the most common means of collecting data.

In forming a questionnaire, you want to carefully choose the questions asked, the wording, and the sequence. Determine what it is you need to know and then choose your questions. Decide if you will have multiple choice questions or if you will require a written answer. Wording is very important. Use simple, direct and unbiased wording. Check the sequence of your questions. The first question should create interest. Ask the most difficult or involved questions at the end.

Decide who is to be surveyed, how many people to use, and how they will be reached. They can be contacted by telephone, mail, or personal interview.

Compile the data and view it objectively. You must remember that marketing is a dynamic and changing process. You must be flexible. Perhaps your original business idea wasn't well received. Did the survey results point the way to a modification of your idea which would make it more acceptable?

You might consider test marketing some samples of your product. Don't use friends or relatives. Their opinions generally aren't objective! Perhaps you could contact the Chamber of Commerce or another civic group to see if you could present samples at one of their meetings. Be sure to include an evaluation form so you can analyze the responses.

You can do a literature search. Spend some time in the library and read the business and trade journals. What seem to be hot, new items and how are they being presented and advertised?

Study the nature of the demand. Are your products or services seasonal? Are the products you provide and the services you offer a fad? Or is there room for growth? Can you think of associated products or services to round out your business?

There are four major groups to whom you can sell: individual consumers, institutions, industry, and government. You may sell retail or wholesale through a manufacturer's representative to reach the retail outlets. If you represent yourself and sell directly to a retail outlet, the store owner may wish to take your product on consignment. This means that you will be paid after the item is sold. You are also liable for any theft or breakage before the sale. Remember that the store is motivated to sell the items it has purchased outright. Your product may not be as prominently displayed as it should be. Sometimes consignment is the only way you will be able to get a product into the marketplace. Be aware of its pitfalls.

Manufacturer's representatives act as middlemen. They present your product to buyers, take orders for you, and forward those orders to you. You will ship the order directly to and receive payment from the store placing the order. For this, the manufacturer's rep will receive a commission from you. The usual rate is 15% to 20% of the wholesale price of the order.

While you may approach individual shops and stores on your own, dealing with sales to institutions and industry usually requires the services of a representative.

You may wish to sell to the Federal Government. Government procurement is big business. As you might expect, paperwork is involved! But if you land a contract with the government for your product or service, it will be well worth the work.

COMPETITION

Once you have generally surveyed the market, found a need, determined how you might fill that need, and thought about the different markets available, you are ready to check out the competition.

Direct competition will be a business offering the same product or service to the same market. Indirect competition is a company with the same product or service but a different target market. You both may be manufacturing the same item, but the other company's product is offered through a catalog while you wish yours to be offered through a retail outlet. There may be a substitute product available to your target market. This is evident in the giftware business where there is keen competition for the consumer's dollar.

On a weekly basis, visit shops selling products similar to yours. How are the items displayed? What colors are used and what packaging catches your eye? What sold during week? What was left and what was marked down? Make a note of the prices of the items. Remember that most stores **keystone** or double the wholesale cost, so you can get an estimate of what the competition's wholesale prices may be.

You want to determine the competitor's image. To what part of the market is he trying to appeal? Can you appeal to the same market in a better way? Or can you find an untapped market?

If you are offering a service, call the competition and ask for job rates, delivery schedules, terms of payment, and discount policies. Since most businesses are wary of competition, you may have to pose as a customer to get the information that you need. Visit your competitor's shop and rate the personnel. Does the shop offer a full line of goods and services? How does the competition promote its service? You will want to make a worksheet for each competitor that you evaluate so that you can draw conclusions about your own entry into the market. You want to be able to determine how to make your business unique.

Your new product or service may be a monopoly. If successful, you can be sure that competition will soon follow. It may be to your advantage to copyright, patent, or secure a trademark for some aspect of your business. This subject is covered in the **Protecting Your Business** section. You must evaluate the competition throughout the life of your business and you may have to adjust your pricing, change your packaging, or change your advertising in order to remain competitive.

TARGET MARKET

Now that you have determined that there is a general need for what you have to offer and have analyzed the competition in terms of how they are filling that need, you are ready to define your target market. You are going to find the group of customers you can best serve.

This will require a trip back to the library to do what is called a **demographic study**. This means that you want answers to the following questions:

> 1. What is the physical location of my target market? Are they urban or rural? Do they live near the ocean or in the mountains? If you offer pack trips into the mountains, you may find your target market among city dwellers who are looking for a new experience. People accustomed to living in the mountains may not see the uniqueness of what you have to offer.

> 2. What is their psychological make-up? What is their self-image and what are their tastes?

> 3. What are their demographics in terms of age, sex, income, culture?

> 4. What are their behavior characteristics? What do they do in their leisure time? Do they have hobbies?

The Census Reports from the Department of Commerce can give you these answers as well as information about economic factors for the area in which your customers live, shop and work.

Your customer surveys and test marketing showed you what your customer needs and wants. You must make that customer feel that your product or service was produced with them in mind. Your target market must be the segment of the market you can service most effectively. Narrow your market in the beginning to the segment which you can effectively handle in terms of your resources, strengths, and weaknesses. You don't want to become too big, too soon and not be able to meet deadlines and production schedules. Later, you can look for growth into new areas.

MARKET PLANNING

Now you are ready to **position** your product or service. Positioning means determining what part of the market you wish to serve and identifying a unique benefit that your product or service has to offer.

PACKAGING DESIGN

One of your first considerations will be your packaging design. Packaging can play a major role in the success of your business. It's what first catches the customer's eye. The L'eggs® container is a good example of eye-catching and memorable packaging. We all associate the container with women's hosiery. Just as you considered the tastes of your target market in the ultimate design of your product, you will make the same considerations in packaging design. Decide what will be the most appealing in terms of size, shape, color, material, and wording. Packaging attracts a great deal of public attention. Be advised of the Fair Packaging and Labeling Act of 1967 which established mandatory labeling requirements. The Food and Drug Administration has strict procedures for the labeling of items falling within their jurisdiction. The packaging guidelines can be obtained by contacting the Agency or by referring to a copy of the regulations in the library.

Your packaging design will be an integral part of the image of your product. It includes your primary package, shipping carton, and label. You may have to redesign in the future to be timely. An example is the special packaging we see at holiday time.

PRICING

Formulas for computing the base price for a product or service were included in the section entitled, **Financing Your Business.** They were used in that section to help you determine if you had adequate financing. Now it is time to refine your price based on the quality of the product or service, the desired image of your company, the prices of competitive products, and the nature of the demand. Adjust your price based on the above consideration. Be aware of what adjustments will do to the figures you used in the pricing formulas. The percentage of the price that is profit will depend on what the traffic will bear. Don't undervalue your product or service.

The major factor considered by a consumer before purchase is the price. You want to price high enough to bring a profit but low enough to appeal to the customer.

ADVERTISING

Advertising presents the message to your customer that your product is a good and desirable one. Tailor your advertising to your target market. What magazines and newspapers do they read? Analyze your competitors' advertising in these publications. The Advertising Department of the publications you choose will tell you how to go about getting your ad designed and published. Your marketing research will have spelled out which television and radio stations and which publications are of interest to your target market. Those are the ones you will use.

DISTRIBUTION

Distribution is the way products are physically transported from producer to consumer and the way services are made available to the public. Distribution is closely related to your target market and your product. If you sell a product by mail, your location is less important than if you own a small store. When you are in a service business, you want to get service to the customer and insure satisfaction. The costs of distribution can affect your production costs.

LOCATION

Location is related to distribution. You must consider how accessible you will be to the public, how best you can meet your customer's needs, and how you can maximize efficiency. You want to be accessible to the most customers for the least cost.

Your location should reflect the image you want to project. A Bed and Breakfast Inn should be in a picturesque setting, not beside a freeway interchange. Even though a market for lodging exists along the freeway, a motel would better suite the image we have of roadside lodging.

Locate the geographic area where there should be a high demand. Look for the location of competitors and for growth potential. Use push pins and a map to mark the locations of competitors. Shade in the areas in which your target market lives, shops and works. Can you locate an untapped area?

Office space for minimal rent is not always the best. There is usually a reason why rent is low. Find out why the space is available, how long it has been vacant, and the history of the previous tenants. If there has been a frequent turnover, it may be considered a "bad location".

Many people prefer a home business. There are many advantages to locating your business in your home. Some of the considerations were discussed in the section entitled, **Financing Your Business.** You can also save on commute costs. This is a practical solution for the parent with childcare concerns. Your time is more flexible and you reduce your financial risk. The I.R.S. and your local Zoning Commission have strict guidelines for home businesses and you should read them carefully.

One of the disadvantages of a home business is the difficulty in projecting a professional image. There will also be family interruptions and you may feel a psychological need to separate home and business. Usually home office space doesn't allow much room for growth.

Some other considerations in a home-based business are the distances to supplier and customers, locations of competitors, future business goals, types of neighborhoods, insurance requirements, and zoning regulations. Zoning laws vary with each city and are mainly concerned with the potential for increased traffic flow, noise pollution, and the change of character of the neighborhood through the use of signs.

Choose your location carefully based on the location of your target market, location of your suppliers, cost, and method of distribution.

TIMING OF MARKET ENTRY

The timing of your product's or service's entry into the market is critical. This area is often overlooked. The reception of a new product can be affected by the seasons, the weather, and the holidays. Early January and September are the best times to mail flyers and catalogs. The major gift shows are held in the summer months (June, July, August) and again in January and February. Most wholesale buying takes place at these shows. You will want to present your products to a manufacturer's rep. well before these dates. November and December are not good months for introducing most new service businesses unless they relate in some way to the holiday season. The spring is a better time to introduce a service.

View the process of market research and planning as detective work. You are on the trail of the elusive "target market" and you won't get paid until you find them! The more clues or information you have, the more successful you will be in finding that customer and having the satisfaction of selling your product or service.

MARKETING RESEARCH WORKSHEET

QUESTIONS	INFO. SOURCE	INFORMATION RESULTS	EFFECT ON PLAN

Marketing Your Business

MARKETING SURVEY
"OCEAN ADVENTURE"

Date_____

Location_____

(please circle answers)

Male/Female   Single/Married/Other

Approximate Age: 0 - 20,   21 - 26,   27 - 35,   36 - over

Do you enjoy outdoor activities?   Yes/No

Do you enjoy ocean and beach activities?   Yes/No

Do you go boating?   Yes/No

Have you ever been in a kayak?   Yes/No

    If yes: a) What did you think of the experience?

                  b) Where were you?

                  c) Were instructors/guides present?

                  d) Did you enjoy the experience?

                  e) Would you be interested in classes on kayaking?

                  f) Would you be interested in kayaking trips?

    If no: a) Would you be interested in kayaking lessons?

Do you have children?

Do you use discount coupons?

What newspapers do you read?_____
_____

What magazines do you read?_____
_____

Your Occupation/Profession_____

Have you heard of **OCEAN ADVENTURE**?   Yes/No

    If yes, source_____

THANK YOU FOR YOUR CONSIDERATION

COMPETITION EVALUATION WORKSHEET

1. Name of Competitor:

2. Location

3. Product:

4. Packaging:

5. Price:

6. Methods of Distribution:

8. Suppliers:

9. Strengths:

10. Weaknesses:

11. Additional information:

Note: A COMPETITION EVALUATION WORKSHEET should be made for each competitor. Keep these records and update them. It pays to continue to rate your competition.

TARGET MARKET WORKSHEET

WHO ARE MY CUSTOMETS?

1. PROFILE

    Economic Level -

    Psychological Make-up -

    Age -

    Sex -

    Income Level -

    Habits -

2. LOCATION:

    Live -

    Work -

    Shop -

3. MARKET SIZE:

4. COMPETITION:

5. OTHER FACTORS:

CUSTOMER NEEDS	WHAT CAN I OFFER?

LOCATION ANALYSIS WORKSHEET

1. Address:

2. Name of Realtor/Contact Persons

3. Former Tenant & Reason for Leaving

4. Square Footage/Cost:

5. Personal Inspection Discoveries:

6. Notes from Walking Tour of Neighborhood:

7. Neighboring Shops:

8. Zoning Regulations:

9. Traffic Patterns:

    for customers-

    for suppliers -

10. Additional Information:

Note: Keep up with changes in the zoning regulations, the traffic patterns, and the business and character of the neighborhood in your location.

SOURCES OF INFORMATION FOR MARKET RESEARCH

FEDERAL GOVERNMENT

1. Bureau of the Budget

   Standard Industrial Classification Manual: This publication lists the SIC numbers issued to major areas of business: for example, the SIC number for piano tuning is #7699.
   Standard Metropolitan Statistical Areas

2. Bureau of the Census

   Issues publications covering demographic and economic surveys.

3. Department of Commerce

   Census of Business: Retail Area Statistics
   Census Tract Manual
   County & City Data Book: This book is updated every three years and contains statistical information on population, education, employment, income, housing, and retail sales.
   County Business Patterns
   Directory of Federal Statistics for Local Areas
   Facts for Marketers
   Measuring Markets: A guide to the use of federal and state statistical data.

4. Small Business Administration

   National Directories for Use in Marketing
   Small Marketers Aids
   Statistics and Maps for Market Analysis

STATE GOVERNMENT

1. State Department of Commerce
2. Office of the Secretary of State
3. State Bookstore

LOCAL GOVERNMENT

1. Regulatory Agencies
2. Urban and Redevelopment Agencies

NON-GOVERNMENT SOURCES

1. Banks
2. Chambers of Commerce
3. Community and State Colleges
4. Entrepreneurs (local business owners)
5. Merchant Associations
6. Retired Entrepreneurs (S.C.O.R.E. counselors may be contacted through the S.B.A.)
7. Suppliers and Wholesalers
8. Trade Associations (Clearing houses for information passing between industry, government, and the general public)

PRINTED MATERIAL

1. Directories which are compiled by Chambers of Commerce and Merchants Associations.

2. Magazines and Journals

    Advertising Age
    Advertising and Sales Promotion
    Business Horizons
    Business Week
    Harvard Business Review
    Industrial Marketing
    Journal of Advertising Research
    Journal of Business
    Journal of Marketing
    Journal of Marketing Research
    Wall Street Journal

3. The Yellow Pages

4. Newspapers

LIBRARIES

1. Publications and Directories available in the Reference Section.

    Business Periodicals Index: A monthly listing of business articles appearing in a wide variety of business publications.
    Directory of Directories: Describes over 9,000 buyer's guides and directories.
    Dun and Bradstreet Directories: List companies alphabetically, geographically, and by product classification.
    Encyclopedia of Associations: Provides information on every major trade and professional association in the United States.
    Marketing Information Guide: Provides a monthly annotated bibliography of marketing information.
    Standard and Poor's Industry Surveys: Updated statistics and analyses of industries.
    Statistical Abstract of the U. S.: Updated annually, provides demographic, economic, and social information.
    U. S. Industrial Outlook: Provides projections of industrial activity.

15. ADVERTISING YOUR BUSINESS

15. ADVERTISING YOUR BUSINESS

Advertising is defined by Webster as "printed or spoken matter that tells about or praises a product, service, etc. publicly so as to make people want to buy it". Advertising is a natural extension of your marketing research and plan. It is the means for getting information about your product or service to the buying public. There are a variety of methods available to accomplish this. Surprisingly enough, all of the methods mentioned in this section are easily accessible, even to the small or home-based business.

MEDIA PUBLICITY can be obtained through interviews, articles and paid ads in newspapers, on radio, and on television.

Newspaper advertising usually reaches a large number of people, has a short life span, is relatively inexpensive, and is easily and quickly changed. Your ad can be placed in a particular section of the paper to reach a selected audience. The cost of your ad will vary according to the circulation areas and the frequency of publication. Ads are available in various sizes and in several formats such as display or classified advertising in regular editions, as inserts to regular editions, and as ads in special editions.

In addition to paid advertising, businesses should definitely consider **publicity.** Publicity is information about you and your product or service. Publicity is not paid advertising. It is free. You can call the Business Editor or Feature Editor of a widely-circulated newspaper in your area and explain your product or service. Before calling, consider what is unique about you and your business. Stress that uniqueness in order to convince the editor that such an article would be of interest to his readers. There are two approaches that can be used when seeking publicity. The first is to request an **interview** either at the newspaper office or in your place of business. The second is to suggest that you contribute a **newspaper article**, complete with photos, telling about some aspect of your business. If one newspaper is not interested, call another. Don't be afraid to approach the media. **You** are the best advertising that you can get.

Radio Advertising is usually local, reaches a preselected audience, can be changed frequently, is limited to brief copy, is relatively expensive, and should be repeated frequently. It is priced according to length of message, time of broadcast, and frequency of broadcast. It is either read live by the announcers or taped in advance. The three biggest complaints about radio ads are that they are noisy, they have idiotic humor, and they lack sincerity. Keep that in mind when you are writing your commercial. Be simple and straight-forward. Another approach to radio coverage of your business would be to offer your services as an expert in your field on a radio talk show. You can answer questions from listeners regarding your business.

Television advertising reaches large marketing areas and may be done in cooperation with national advertisers. It is relatively expensive and limited to brief copy. Television advertising is usually highly professional and priced according to length of message, time of broadcast, frequency of broadcast, time of year, and whether or not the station is an independent or member of a network. Don't discount Cable Television. This medium is becoming very useful to the small business owner. If television advertising costs are prohibitive, you should consider approaching the television news department from the publicity point of view. Call the television stations in your area. Ask the receptionist which shows have guests. Ask for the name of the person that is in charge of securing those guests. Follow up by contacting that person and promote yourself in a most professional way. Your business may qualify for a Public Service Announcement (known in the trade as a PSA). This is a good way to announce classes or to publicize any meetings at which you may be a guest speaker.

DISPLAYS, COMMUNITY INVOLVEMENT, and **NETWORKING** offer other means of advertising.

Displays may be set up at community-oriented functions such as city fairs, community meetings and civic events. This is a good way to present your product or service to the buying public.

Community involvement can be a valuable means of advertising. Membership in civic organizations can pave the way to being a guest speaker. Active membership, alone, affords you an excellent opportunity for networking.

Networking is the exchange of ideas and information that takes place every day in your life. You are going to direct that exchange to your benefit and the benefit of those around you. The more you meet with people and network, the more you will be able to promote your business, to learn more about the business community around you, and to become more self-confident. Membership in the Chamber of Commerce is an excellent means of accomplishing this goal.

TRADE SHOWS and **EXHIBITS** allow you to take advantage of promotional campaigns that would be too expensive for a small business to undertake alone. You can request listings of trade events from malls and convention centers. Participation in trade shows and membership in trade organizations give you visibility within your occupational field. These shows are usually attended only by those interested in your particular business or service. This is an excellent way to reach your target market.

DIRECT MAIL as a campaign has as one of its elements the development of a brochure to advertise your business. Brochures can be expensive. Therefore, their distribution should be carefully and effectively planned. Mailing lists are available for rent in order to reach your market. Sources of mailing lists can be found in the library. Brochures can be mailed, delivered door-to-door, or handed out at special events. They contain more information than a classified ad and, if they are well-done, can be a very successful way of presenting your business. For little additional cost, your brochure can be typeset by a printer for a more professional look.

YELLOW PAGES should not be overlooked as a means of advertising. Every person with a telephone has a copy of the Yellow Pages. It is a fact that they are one of the most widely-used forms of advertising. One small home-business owner states that 50% of her customers in any given week are new clients who have found her business through the Yellow Pages. The telephone company advertising staff is very knowledgeable and will give you help in designing an ad which will present your business in an effective manner. Be aware that directories are published at various times of the year. Call the phone company to determine the publication deadlines.

DISCOUNTS are an excellent way to get additional customers. Discounts can be given to customers who bring referrals. They may also be offered through coupons and brochures. Everyone likes to think that they are saving money.

PROMOTIONAL GIMMICKS may take the form of T-shirts, pens, key rings, plastic shopping bags, calendars, balloons, and bumper stickers. The most effective gimmicks are useful items. The gimmick should be appropriate to the business it's representing. For example, a logo or business name on a T-shirt is an effective way of advertising a business dealing with the out-of-doors, such as a bicycle shop or a kite maker. Pens would be good for someone who manufactures notecards and stationery. Balloons could represent a company specializing in children's items. Be creative in your use of this advertising form.

SUMMARY

The forms of advertising chosen by you must be evaluated for effectiveness. As a new business, your advertising budget will probably be limited. Choose the form of advertising that will best reach your target market. Ask your customers how they found out about your business. Use this information to compile an **Advertising Response Record.** A sample form is at the end of this section. From this information, determine which has been the most effective means of advertising for your business. Eliminate those methods which have not proved effective and divert those funds to increase your advertising in the areas which will give you the best results.

After evaluating the different methods of advertising, work up an individual plan for your business. A sample of such a plan, which was made for one of our clients, follows this section.

ADVERTISING IDEAS FOR OCEAN ADVENTURES

RADIO: Contact local radio stations and ask for their procedure in securing talk show guests. Inform them of your area of expertise and stress the uniqueness of what you offer and the high interest of the public in what your business is doing. Suggest that you can relate kayaking experiences you have had and would enjoy taking listener calls.

NEWSPAPER: Contact the Sports Editor, Business Editor, Travel Editor and slant your article idea according to their areas of interest. The Sports Editor would be interested in an article about "The Sport of Ocean Kayaking". The Business Editor may want to cover a new and unique business developing within the area covered by his newspaper. The Travel Editor will be interested in an article entitled, "Kayaking to Baja". Have black and white photos available of the different aspects of your business.

Consider publishing an ad in the business section. Trained people at the newspaper can advise you about placement and size of ad. Be prepared to give the who, what, why, where, and how of the class or trip you will be offering.

TELEVISION: Contact television studios in your area and inquire about their format for securing talk show guests. Suggest that you could demonstrate the use of a kayak for their viewers, tell about trips you have taken, and demonstrate safety techniques. Perhaps, the host would be willing to be televised while taking a basic lesson!

Cable television also offers opportunities for coverage and less expensive advertising. Explore this resource.

Public Broadcasting Stations often have televised auctions as fund-raisers. Consider donating your Basic Paddling Course as one of the items offered for auction. This would be invaluable advertising.

DISPLAY: Create a display featuring photos of your trips and classes, copies of any publicity you have received, a kayak and the gear related to using, and have plenty of brochures and business cards on hand. Be prepared to answer questions regarding your business. Community affairs such as fairs and festivals usually offer space for this type of display. This format can also be used as an **EXHIBIT** at trade shows such as a Travel Show or Sports and Boating Show. These larger events are usually held in sports arenas or convention facilities.

COMMUNITY INVOLVEMENT: Join the Chamber of Commerce! This excellent group will afford you a forum for speaking as well as being a great networking group.

Consider working with a **Scout Council.** You could counsel in kayaking, water safety, and/or marine studies. This offers a new area for networking.

Look into teaching through the **YMCA**. Basic skills courses could be taught through the Y with a discount given to Y students who continue study.

BROCHURE: Make your message personal and stress your product or service. A brochure should show how your business is different from the competition and stress the advantages of dealing with you to the customer (see brochure in this section).

YELLOW PAGES AD: Yellow page advertising does work! Discuss placement and category with the staff in the Advertising Department of the Yellow Pages. They will be able to advise you.

PROMOTIONAL GIMMICKS: T-shirts with your name and logo could be given to those attending your classes and going on your trips. This would seem to be an appropriate promotional tool; active, outdoor people wear t-shirts and you will get good exposure this way.

Advertising is a continuing process. Be prepared to follow up on all leads. Have brochures ready to be mailed when you receive an inquiry. People get distracted and lose interest if their requests aren't handled promptly. Consider discounts for groups and referrals.

Advertising Your Business

PRESS RELEASE FORM

SOURCE INFORMATION

Name, address, phone number of person to call for more info.

RELEASE DATE

For immediate release or specify date to be published.

HEADLINE

(Centered in Capital Letters)

BASIC FACTS

(Who, What, When, Where, How)

FOR MORE INFORMATION: Be sure to include name and address and/or phone number in the article so that the reader can obtain additional information.

OUT OF YOUR MIND AND INTO THE MARKETPLACE

ADVERTISING RESPONSE RECORD

TYPE OF AD	DATE	COST	CIRCULATION	NO. RESPONSES	INCOME GENERATED

16.

BUSINESS PLANNING

THE KEY TO YOUR SUCCESS

16. BUSINESS PLANNING

THE KEY TO YOUR SUCCESS

One of the principal reasons most businesses fail is the lack of an adequate plan. When the concept of Business Plan is considered, three critical facts always emerge:

1. All lending institutions require a Business Plan
2. All businesses need a Business Plan
3. FEW BUSINESS OWNERS KNOW HOW TO WRITE A BUSINESS PLAN!!!!

We have been teaching business workshops to entrepreneurs and have found that no task seems to cause more consternation and dread than that of facing the ominous task of preparing a Business Plan. In fact, most new business owners will forge ahead without one, sure that a good idea, enthusiasm, and the desire to achieve their goal will be enough to ensure business success. Unfortunately, there is a major flaw in this type of thinking. Most of us are not proficient in all phases of our particular industry, and therefore do not have enough knowledge to make the best decisions and to see what changes will have to be implemented in the future.

PURPOSES

There are three main purposes for writing a business plan. The first, and most important, is to serve as a guide during the lifetime of your business. It is the blueprint of your business and will serve to keep you on the right track. To be of value, your plan must be kept up-to-date. If you will spend the time to plan ahead, many pitfalls will be avoided and needless frustrations will be eliminated. Secondly, the business plan is a requirement if you are planning to seek loan funds. It will provide potential lenders with detailed information on all aspects of the company's past and current operations and make future projections. Thirdly, the business plan details how the desired investment or loan will further the company's goals. Every banker wants to know how the loan will improve the worth of your company. It will detail how the money will be used and back up your figures with estimates from suppliers.

FORMAT

When you write your business plan, you will want to include detailed information in a particular format. The one we propose includes the following sections:

- **COVERSHEET**
  The title page of your plan.
  Contains name, address, telephone no., etc.

- **STATEMENT OF PURPOSE**
  The thesis statement of your business plan.
  Formulated after writing your plan.

- **TABLE OF CONTENTS**
  Listing of contents of your plan.
  Used to locate areas addressed in plan.

- **BUSINESS SECTION**
  Information on your industry, in general.
  Information on your business, in particular.

- **MARKETING SECTION**
  Information on your total market.
  Emphasis on your target market.

- **FINANCIAL DOCUMENTS**
  Records showing past and current finances.
  Records projecting future finances.

- **SUPPORTING DOCUMENTS**
  Documents that back up statements and decisions made in the three main parts of your plan.

REVISION OF YOUR BUSINESS PLAN

If your Business Plan is going to be effective either to the business or to a potential lender, it will be necessary for you to update it on a regular basis. Changes are constantly taking place in your business. Therefore, revision is an on-going process. You, as the owner, must be aware of the changes in your industry, your market, and your community. You must determine what revisions are needed and be responsible for implementing those changes.

INFORMATION RESOURCES FOR WRITING A BUSINESS PLAN

There are many resources available to aid you in the writing of your plan. If you are skillful in the use of the resource section of the library, there is a wealth of information available on almost every phase of most industries. The Small Business Administration has many useful publications to aid you in preparing your plan. You might also consider utilizing SCORE (Senior Corps of Retired Executives) to help you get started with a new business. There are many workshops available at a private and public educational institutions.

ANATOMY OF A BUSINESS PLAN

We have written a textbook that will provide you with a step-by-step format that is simple, concise, and easy-to-understand. It will help you to create your business plan. You can always hire a professional to write it for you, but if you will take the time and effort to do it yourself, you will be well on the road to success. You will be a business owner with a thorough understanding of your venture and you will have greatly increased its potential for growth and profits.

17. FOR MORE INFORMATION

17. FOR MORE INFORMATION

The following resources are listed as supplements to the sources cited in the text. When requesting information, use your company letterhead and enclose a SASE (self-addressed, stamped envelope).

AMERICAN COUNCIL FOR THE ARTS
570 Seventh Avenue
New York, NY 10018

This organization provides information and technical assistance in the arts. Publishes books, manuals, and a magazine, American Arts. Free catalog lists material available.

AMERICAN CRAFTS COUNCIL
401 Park Avenue South
New York, NY 10016

Non-profit organization serving professional craftsmen, artists, and designers, Request information on publications and membership benefits.

ARTISTS MARKET
Writer's Digest
9933 Alliance Road
Cincinnati, OH 45242

Book which lists over 3,000 buyers of art work including book publishers, stores and greeting card companies. Issued annually. Also publishes:

Songwriter's Market
Photographer's Market
Writer's Market

ATLAS PEN AND PENCIL CORPORATION
3040 N. 29th Avenue
Hollywood, FL 33022

Free catalog listing promotional gimmicks for use in advertising.

BUREAU OF CONSUMER PROTECTION
Division of Special Statutes
6th and Pennsylvania Ave, N.W.
Washington, DC 20580

Write for information related to your specific business.

CONSUMER PRODUCTS AND SAFETY COMMISSION
Bureau of Compliance
5401 Westbard Avenue
Bethesda, MD 20207

Request catalog of booklets available: For example
- **The Federal Hazardous Substances Act**
- **Consumer Products Safety Act of 1972**
- **Flammable Fabrics Act**

THE CRAFTS REPORT
700 Orange Street
P.O. Box 1992
Wilmington, DE 19899

Monthly publication covering all aspects of the professional craft field. Classified ad section for buyers and sellers. Annual subscription rate: $17.50.

DOVER PUBLICATIONS
31 E. 2nd Street
Mineola, N.Y. 11501

Send for a free catalog of books which include copyright-free designs.

THE DRAWING BOARD
256 Regal Row
P.O. Box 220505
Dallas, TX 75222

Send for free catalog of office supplies, business forms, and labels.

FEDERAL TRADE COMMISSION
Division of Legal and Public Records
Washington, DC 20580

Request trade practice rules applicable to your business. Examples:
The Jewelry Industry
The Hand Knitting Yarn Industry

FOOD AND DRUG ADMINISTRATION
5600 Fishers Lane
Rockville, MD 20857

Send for requirements governing packaging and labeling of food and food-related products.

GEORGE LITTLE MANAGEMENT, INC.
2 Park Avenue, Suite 1100
New York, NY 10016

Organizer and promoter of wholesale trade shows. Write for calendar of shows and registration information.

INTERNAL REVENUE SERVICE
Washington, DC 20224

Request list of publications such as:
Tax Guide for Small Business #334
Business Use of Your Home #587

NATIONAL BUREAU OF STANDARDS
Technical Building B 167
Standard Development Services Section
Washington, DC 20234

Information on special labeling required for products made of special metals such as gold and silver.

NEBS, INC.
500 Main Street
Groton, MA 01471-0002

Send for free catalog of office supplies, business forms, and labels.

POLK MAILING LIST CATALOG
R.L. Polk and Co.
Special List Marketing
3050 Holcombe Bridge Road
Norcross, GA 30071

Request information on mailing lists available for rent.

REP WORLD
Albee-Campbell, Inc.
806 Penn Avenue
Sinking Spring, PA 19608

Information on selling through manufacturer's reps.

SMALL BUSINESS REPORTER
Bank of America
Department 3120
P.O. Box 37000
San Francisco, CA 94137

Source of practical up-to-date information for small business. Send for free list of list of titles; there is a charge for each publication..
    Sample titles:
Financing Small Business
Understanding Financial Statements

SUPERINTENDENT OF DOCUMENTS
U.S. Government Printing Office
Washington, DC 20402

Request subject bibliography listings. There are fees for most publications. Sample titles are:

For Women: Managing Your Own Business
Handbook for Small Business
Managing for Profits
Inventory Management
Evaluating Money Sources

U.S. DEPARTMENT OF COMMERCE

Office of Consumer Affairs
Washington, DC 20233

Offers free booklets such as:

Product Warranties
Advertising, Packaging, and Labeling

U.S. DEPARTMENT OF LABOR
200 Constitution Avenue, N.W.
Washington, DC 20210

Request catalog of publications such as:

Raising Money and Running Your Own Business

For More Information

U.S. SMALL BUSINESS ADMINISTRATION
1441 L Street, N.W.
Washington, DC 20416

Request order forms and listings for the SBA series called Management Aids, Starting Out Series, and Small Business Bibliographies. There is a small charge for most publications. Sample listings follow:

- **The ABC's of Borrowing MA 1.001**
- **What is the Best Selling Price? MA1.002**
- **Getting the Facts about Income Tax Reporting MA1.014**
- **Keeping Records in Small Business MA1.017**
- **Business Plan for Small Manufacturer's MA2.007**
- **Factors in Considering a Shopping Center Location MA 2.017**
- **Home Business SBB 2**
- **Ideas into Dollars (Investors' Guide) SBB 91**
- **Selling by Mail Order SOS 0149**
- **Radio-Television Repair Shop SOS 0104**
- **Starting an Independent Consulting Practice SOS 0204**

INDEX

A

Active business, 27
Advertising, 159
Advertising plan sample, 166-167
Advertising response record, 169
Advertising your Business, 159-170
    Direct Mail, 163
    Discounts, 163
    Displays, community involvement, 162
    and networking, 162
    Media publicity, 161
    Promotional gimmicks, 163
    Trade shows, exhibits, 163
    Yellow Pages, 163
Applying for a business license, 54
Applying for a DBA, 57
Applying for a resale tax number, 67
Assets, 108

B

Balance Sheet, 108
    Balance sheet sample, 127
    Explanation of categories, 126
Bank Account, 81
Brochures, 14
    Sample brochures, 17, 18
Business cards, 13
    Sample business cards, 23
Business license, 53
Business names, 9
Business planning, 171-176
    Anatomy of a Business Plan, 175
    Format, 174
    Informational Resources, 175
    Purposes, 173
    Revisions, 174
By-laws of incorporation, 43

C

CA sales and use tax form, 75, 76
Capital accounts, 108
Cash to be paid out work-sheet, 95
Certificate of Incorporation, 42
Checkbook, 82, 107
Checking account, 81
Choosing a bank, 81
    Worksheet, 83
Choosing a Business Name, 7-10
Choosing a printer, 15
Common deductible expenses, 104, 110, 111
Community involvement, 162
Competition, 145
    Competition evaluation form, 153
Copyright classification, 29
Copyright notice, 28
Copyright office, 33
Copyright resources, 33
Corporation, 40
    Advantages, 41
    Disadvantages, 41
Cost of goods sold, 90
Cost of services provided, 90
Credits, 105
Customer records, 107

D

DBA, 10, 57
Debits, 105
Deductible Business Expense, 110, 111
Demographic study, 146
Depreciation, 89, 106, 110, 111
Direct mail, 163
Disclosure letter, 27
Discounts, 163
Displays, 162

Distribution, 148
Draw, 90

E

End of Year, 107
Envelopes, 14
Estimated taxes, 112, 113
Exhibits, 163
Expenses, 104

F

Fictitious Business Name Statement, 57
Fictitious name, 55
    Benefits, 58
    Certificate publication, 58
    Renewal, 58
Finding a Business, 1-6
Files, 107
Financial statement form, 96, 97
Financing your Business, 85-100
Formula for manufacturers, 91
    Examples of use, 99
For More Information, 177-186

G

General Journal, 105
    Sample page, 120
General recordkeeping schedule, 132, 133

H

Home-based business deductions, 110, 149
Home Business, 61-64
Hourly rate formula, 90
    Examples of use, 98

I

Income, 104
Income Statement, 108, 128
    Sample, 128, 129
Insurance, 89, 137
Insurance Fact Sheet, 139
Interests, 3, 4
Inventory record, 106
    Inventory record form, 123

J

Journal, 27

K

Keeping records, 101-134
    Balance sheet, 108, 127
    Capital accounts, 108
    Checkbook, 107
    Customer records, 107
    Expenses, 104
    Files, 107
    General ledger, 105, 120
    Income, 104
    Inventory record, 106, 123
    Petty cash record, 105, 122
    Recordkeeping schedule, 132, 133
    Setting up your records, 104
    Tax regulations, 104
    Types of recordkeeping, 103
Keystone, 92, 145

L

Legal Structures, 35-50
    By-Laws, 43
    Certificate of incorporation, 42
    Corporation, 40
    Partnership, 38
    Partnership agreement, 39

Sole proprietorship, 37
SubChapter S, 41
Letterheads, 14
Liabilities, 108
Location, 53
Location analysis worksheet, 155
Log, 27
Logos, 14

M

Manufacturer's reps, 145
Marketing research worksheet, 151
Marketing survey sample, 152
Marketing your Business, 141-158
- Marketing plan, 147
  - Advertising, 148
  - Distribution, 148
  - Location, 148
  - Packaging design, 147
  - Pricing, 147
  - Timing of market entry, 149
- Market research, 144-149
  - Check out the competition, 145
  - Identify target market, 146
  - Survey the market, 144
  - Sources of information, 156, 157
Media flyer, 19, 20
Media publicity, 161

N

Networking, 162
Newspaper advertising, 161
Press release form, 168

O

Obtaining a Seller's Permit, 65-78
Office of Name Availability, 42
Operating expenses, 88

P

Packaging design, 147
Partnership, 38
- Advantages, 38
- Disadvantages, 39
Partnership agreement, 39
- Example, 47-49
Patents, 30
Patent and Trademark Office, 30
Petty cash record, 105
- Sample petty cash form, 122
Presenting your Business, 11-24
Press release form, 168
Pricing, 90, 147
Pricing formulas, 90, 91
- Examples of use, 98, 99
Profit and loss sample sheet, 121
Promotional gimmicks, 163
Proof of publication, DBA, 60
Protecting your Business, 25-34
- Copyright, 28
- Patent, 30
- Resources, 33
- Trademark, 29
Publicity, 161

Q

Questionnaire, 144
- Sample, 152

R

Radio advertising, 162
Recordkeeping, 101-134
Recordkeeping schedule, 132, 133
Records retention table, 119
Registering a Fictitious Name, 55-60
- Benefit, 58
- Certificate publication, 58

Renewal, 58
Rent or mortgage payments, 88
Reporting sales tax, 68
Resale certificate, 68
Resale tax number, 67
    Application form, 71, 72

S

Salaries, 58
Sales sheet examples, 17, 18
Sales tax, 67
Sales tax flow chart, 77
Sales tax return, 75, 76
Secretary of State, 42
Securing a Business License, 51-54
Selecting your Insurance, 135-140
Seller's permit, 67
Setting a price, 90
Setting up a Bank Account, 79-84
Setting up your records, 104
Skills, 3, 4
Skills and Interest Worksheet, 5
Small Business Administration, 156
Sole Proprietorship, 37
    Advantages, 37
    Disadvantages, 38
Sources of cash worksheet, 94
Sources of information
    for market research, 156, 157
Start-up costs, 88
State Board of Equalization, 67
    Application, 67
Sub Chapter S, 41
Summary of revenue and
    expenses form, 125
Superintendent of Documents, 33
Survey the market, 144

T

Target market, 146
    Target market worksheet, 154
Tax form samples, 112-118
    Estimated tax computation, 112
    1040 ES, 113
    Form 1040, Schedule C, 114, 115
    Form 1040, Schedule SE, 116
    Form 4562, 117, 118
Tax regulations, 104
Taxes, 88
Television advertising, 162
Test market, 144
Timing of market entry, 149
Trademark, 29
Trademark resources, 33
Trademark symbol, 30
Tradeshows, 163
Travel, 89
    Travel expense form, 124
Types of recordkeeping, 103

U

U.S. Small Business Administration, 156
Utilities, 89

V

Venture capital, 88

W

Wage, 90

Y

Yellow Pages, 163